Mistakes Retirees Make with Their Finances

And How to Avoid Them

Learn the Issues That Are Often Not Discussed Yet Are Important To Your Financial Security:

Time Horizon
Long-Term Care
Mutual Funds
Stocks
Annuities
Income Investing
IRAs
Estate Planning

Presented by
Michael Pultro, CSA, RFC
Certified Senior Advisor
Registered Financial Consultant
Registered Principal
FFP Securities, Inc. Member NASD/SIPC
FFP Advisory Sevices, Inc.

The articles contained in this book were written by a well-known financial educator.

Contents

FIGURES

TABLES

Introduction

Have you noticed that when you read information about investing in finances, the advice is usually targeted at someone preparing for his or her retirement? Have you found advice that is designed for someone close to retirement or already retired?

In this book, I will cover the issues most important to individuals over the age of 60. In fact, this book provides helpful information about how to avoid the most common and costly financial mistakes. I will focus on the following topics:

Time Horizon
Many seniors think that their investing time horizon is 10 or 20 years. However, the life expectancy data strongly suggests that today's 60 year-olds need to plan for the next 20 to 30 years and organize their finances accordingly. I will share that data with you shortly.

Long-Term Care
Although most seniors don't like to think about the issue of long-term care, it's a reality affecting approximately 50% of individuals over age 65, so you must be prepared. This chapter highlights the most effective and affordable ways to complete your health protection program.

Mutual Funds
America has a love affair with mutual funds. It seems that ***Money Magazine***, CNBC and the Internet have convinced investors that they know everything about selecting mutual funds. In this chapter, I will discuss the issues not often addressed by mutual fund companies and most financial advisors. These issues can have a lasting impact on your fund's performance and profitability.

Stocks
Several studies have shown that most investors are poor investors. This chapter will drop the hype and frenzy created by the press and present actual facts that drive stock market performance. This information is designed to help you become a far richer investor.

Annuities
Annuities are a popular investment for mature investors looking for tax-deferred options and the principal safety provided by fixed annuities. However, making incorrect choices and failing to understand how to withdraw funds can be quite costly.

Income Investing
As you grow older and no longer draw a paycheck, income from your investments will become more important to you. Therefore, I will devote a chapter to the issue of obtaining income from your investments to potentially increase your lifestyle comfort.

IRAs
Many people give little thought to naming beneficiaries, figuring out how their IRAs get treated for estate purposes and fully understanding income tax and estate tax issues. I have included a chapter which discusses the reasons why removing money from an IRA early can make tax sense.

Estate Planning
Mistakes in this area are expensive. The estate tax rates start at 37% and rise to 50%. It's the most expensive tax many people will ever pay that could possibly be avoided or minimized with a few changes. However, they don't make the necessary changes, and as a result, the taxes are paid following their deaths, when it's too late and nothing can be done.

Many of the topics discussed in this book may be similar to ideas mentioned by your financial advisor. However, many of these ideas may represent issues that some financial advisors do not like to discuss. I think that it's important for you to be an educated investor and have a good understanding about what you're doing with your money.

Often, when you're making an investment, an advisor will tell you about the benefits, sometimes omitting risks or issues about what happens to the investment over time or the tax ramifications. In this book, you will learn about some of those issues. Let's dig in.

1

TIME HORIZON

Have you ever thought to yourself, "Do I have enough money to last?" When people get very concerned about having enough money and wanting to keep it close to the vest, they typically make conservative short-term investment decisions.

They invest in conservative income investments such as short-term CDs, fixed annuities and short-term bonds. As people age, they get more security-oriented. Did you ever notice that many senior housing communities are built as gated facilities? I notice how my mother talked about security issues more frequently as she got older—both monetary and otherwise. While that's natural, it can lead to some costly investing mistakes. Let me explain.

If I told a 75-year-old, "I recommend that you buy a ten-year bond," what do you think they might say to me? They'd say that a ten-year investment is too long. Instead, they may want to buy a six-month CD.

As I write this, I see in the December 17, 2001 issue of ***Barron's*** that a six-month CD nationally averages 1.92%, while a ten-year federally backed mortgage note is paying 5.2%—a 175% difference between those two numbers! So, the person who opts for the six-month CD versus a ten-year federally backed mortgage note gives up about 175% more income. Does that make sense to do? A lot of people do it.

What I've noticed is that as people age, they keep investing for shorter and shorter time horizons. Bad mistake. So, I'd like to give you a rule—your investments should be made for as long as you will live.[1]

In the long run, you only have two choices with money—either you are going to outlive your money or your money is going to outlive you. Which scenario would you rather have happen to you? Although most people would like both to expire on the same day; that's unlikely.

The only sensible choice is to have your money and your investments outlive you. Don't buy six-month CDs unless you think you will be dying in five months. Some statistics might help us determine how long you'll be around. The following table shows how long people live.

Table 1.1
Life Expectancies

Current Age	Life Expectancy
65-68	85
69-72	86
73-75	87
76-77	88
78-80	89
81-82	90
83-84	91
85-86	92
90	95
100	103

Life Expectancy Tables; ***2001 IRS Publication 590***

[1] Note the differences between CDs and federally backed mortgage notes: CDs are FDIC insured, mortgage notes are not. Prices of federally backed mortgage notes will fluctuate and if sold prior to maturity, there may be a profit or loss, while early redemptions of CDs cause an early withdrawal penalty. Payments from mortgage notes may contain taxable interest and principal payments which are not taxable. The term of a mortgage note is indeterminate as the mortgages can be paid back at any time while CDs have fixed maturities.

The average person who is now 73 years old will live to age 87. That's 14 years. So, if I advised the average 73-year-old to buy a 15-year bond, that would not be too long. If you understand what I am saying—make sure your money lasts as long as you do—try to secure long-term investments, which tend to pay more (with rare exceptions). The best way to preserve your principal is to make your money earn as much as possible, because the more it earns, the less chance you're ever going to have to touch the capital.

Please think about that carefully. The more you earn, the less chance you will ever need to touch your capital. Therefore, the perceived risk in making longer-term fixed income investments, in fact, reduces your risk because you have more income. You have a bigger financial cushion.[2]

If your expenses are $30,000 a year and your income is $28,000, where does the other $2000 come from? It comes out of your principal. But if your expenses are $30,000 and your income is $40,000, you are going to be adding to your principal. You won't need to touch your principal. The best way to preserve principal or not touch it at all is to make sure your investments earn as much as possible. And you can't do that with short-term investments. So, let me finish by telling you some good news and some bad news.

The life expectancy table is probably too conservative. This table is historical and reflects the longevity of people born decades ago. In other words, based on historical fact, a person who reaches age 73 on average will live until age 87. For those of you reading this book, those numbers are even higher. That's because I don't have your history yet. The

[2] Longer-term fixed income investments fluctuate more than short-term investments. Therefore, I recommend that investors hold fixed income investments until maturity when face value is returned by the issuer. In such a case, the fluctuations during the term will have no effect on the investor's income nor impact the ultimate amount of principal that he/she receives.

table on this page contains data for people who have already died. But the life expectancy trend is still accurate today. The table shows what's happened to life expectancy and what continues to occur. The bad news (financially anyway) is that life expectancy keeps increasing!

Figure 1.1
The Rising Tide of Life Expectancies (1900-1997)

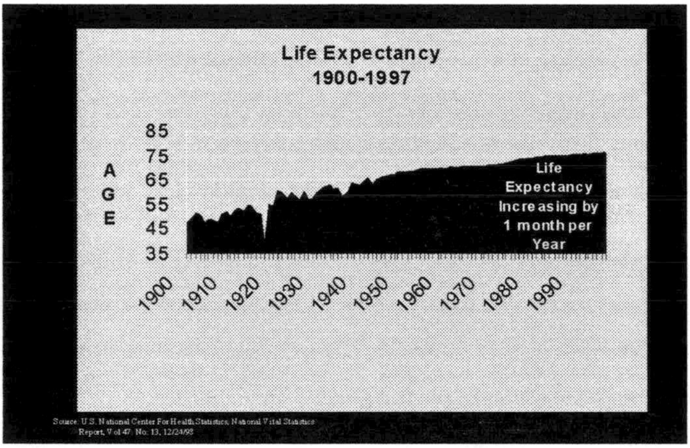

In 1850, the average person lived approximately 37 years. In 1900, that number rose to 47 years. Notice that this chart keeps climbing at about one month of additional life expectancy per year. It doesn't seem to slow down. Doctors are very good at getting us to live longer. So, that's the good news. The bad news is that you need more money. It's a double-edged sword.

I'll show you something amazing. I saw an ad in a magazine and I had to cut it out. (I've removed the company name from the ad.) Is that absolutely amazing when you read it that way? You just never think of it that way, but it is startling. So. The point is, plan to be around a long time.

Figure 1.2
An Insurance Company Ad

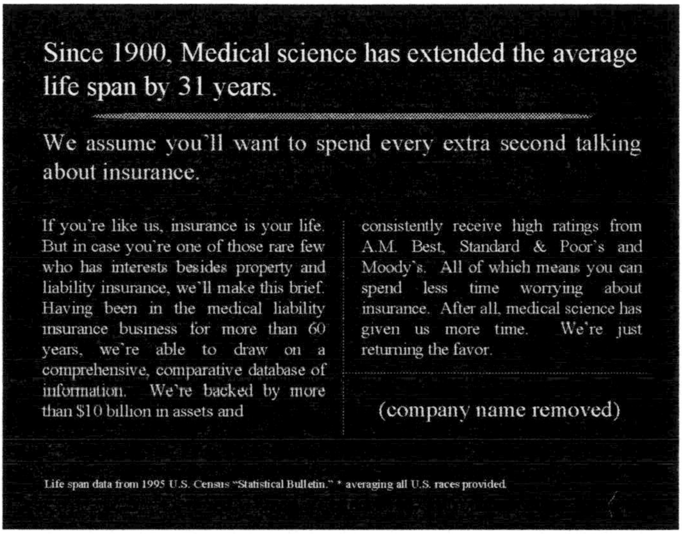

Research is ongoing to lengthen the human life span. A lot of money and expertise is being invested to cure diseases that shorten life. There is evidence that cell biologists Drs. Jerry Shay and Woodring Wright have discovered that the tips of chromosomes may hold the beginning of hope for cancer patients and people hoping to defy old age.

Scientists Extend the Life Span Of Human Cells
(Reprinted with permission from the University of Texas Southwestern Medical Center).

DALLAS — Jan. 13, 1998 — Researchers at UT Southwestern Medical Center at Dallas and their colleagues at Geron Corp., Menlo Park, Calif., say they have figured out how to overcome the mechanisms that control cellular aging and extend the life span of human cells.

In the Jan. 16 issue of ***Science****, Drs. Woodring*

Wright and Jerry Shay, UT Southwestern professors of cell biology and neuroscience, and their collaborators report finding that the enzyme telomerase — which UT Southwestern scientists call a "cellular fountain of youth" — causes human cells grown in the laboratory to retain their "youth" and continue to divide long past the time when they normally stop dividing.

Normal human cells have a limited capacity to proliferate. After a certain finite number of cell divisions, time on the biological clock runs out; the cells "age" and stop dividing. Time remaining in a cell's life correlates with the length of the telomeres — repeated sequences of DNA on the ends of chromosomes that protect the tips from degradation. In normal cells, telomeres shorten with each cell division. Although some have thought that this telomere shortening might be the biological clock's control mechanism, the hypothesis was controversial. The research now proves that human cells grow older each time they divide because their telomeres shorten.

Specialized reproductive cells and most cancer cells appear to divide indefinitely. They contain the enzyme telomerase, which adds back telomeric DNA to the ends of chromosomes. Most normal cells do not have this enzyme.

"We have found that cellular aging can be bypassed by the introduction of the catalytic component of the immortalizing enzyme telomerase," Shay said. "The expression of telomerase LIFE SPAN – 2 in normal human cells should extend their life span indefinitely. From a basic research point of view, we could begin to replace the abnormal tumor-cell lines now being used to study biochemical and physiological aspects of growth and differentiation with normal, yet immortal cell lines."

The scientists introduced telomerase into normal

human cells to see if the cells' life spans could be prolonged. The cells with telomerase extended the length of their telomeres, divided for 20 additional generations past the time they normally would stop dividing and are continuing to divide. The cells also grew and divided in a normal manner, giving rise to normal cells with the normal number of chromosomes. By all accounts these cells had found their fountain of youth.

"The extension of normal cell life span in a youthful state by telomerase is a dramatic confirmation of the telomere hypothesis and one that presents numerous opportunities for biotechnology and medicine," said Dr. Calvin Harley, Geron vice president and chief scientific officer.

One immediate use of finding that telomere shortening controls cellular aging may be in the area of producing engineered products in human cells. "Instead of using uncharacterized primary human-cell cultures to produce vaccines or other biological products, one should now be able to produce products in a re-engineered normal human cell-type that does not change," Wright said.

"This research raises the possibility that we could take a patient's own cells, rejuvenate them, then modify the cells as needed and give them back to the patient to treat a variety of genetic and other diseases," Wright said. "The potential long-term applications are simply staggering."

Other investigators on the project included Drs. Andrea Bodnar, Maria Frolkis, Choy-Pik Chiu, Gregg B. Morin, Calvin Harley and Serge Lichtsteiner of Geron Corp.; and Drs. Michel Ouellette and Shawn Holt, research fellows in UT Southwestern's Department of Cell Biology and Neuroscience. The research was funded in part by the National Institutes of Health.

The investigators' website can be found at:

www.swmed.edu/home_pages/cellbio/shay/

Aging in America

by Ron Kennedy, M.D., Santa Rosa, California

(Reprinted with permission from Ron Kennedy, M.D., www.medical-library.net).

What follows is an overview of where we will be in the next century with aging and the results of aging in America, barring any changes in the way we approach health care in America.

The Situation We Face

By 2011 the first baby-boomers will be ready for retirement and by the year 2025, as the baby-boomers finally mature, there will be twice as many people over 65 as there will be teenagers. In that year we will need at least 31,000 geriatricians, compared to the 1,000 we have today. Right now there are over 70,000 centenarians; by 2006 there will be 100,000 and by 2025 there will be two million.

Right now, today, there are 100 million people with degenerative diseases: cancer, cardiovascular disease and arthritis. That number will double early in the next century.

In the next five years we will see a 14% increase in amount of medical care needed. By 2001 Medicare will be completely bankrupt and by 2029 Social Security will be bankrupt. The children and grandchildren of the baby-boomer generation will have to work 12-hour days to support their parents and grandparents. Alternatively, the older generations may be cut loose to survive on their own as best they can, a sort of modern day economic survival of the fittest.

However, increasingly common preventive health

practices will dramatically slow the expression of aging in our society. Many more "seniors" are no longer feeling old, do not want to "retire," and are remaining active and productive. This group will grow dramatically in coming years and this will change the economic equation completely as people who were expected to be recipients continue to be contributors.

The intense research into the causes of aging is reaching the public consciousness. A recent ***Time Magazine*** *cover story explains part of that research in detail. If* ***Time Magazine*** *writes about it even main stream medicine must have heard about it and will have to extend to this new brand of medicine grudging acknowledgment. Even barring any further advances, the upper limits of what is possible in longevity are quite unknown. In the first quartile of the next century we will surely see people living to 150 or beyond with great vitality.*

What is making this possible is a shift in the paradigm of aging. Increasingly, people are no longer willing to roll over and accept an early death as inevitable. What was inevitable in the old paradigm is not even acceptable in the new. Now we see aging as not just one thing, but rather a complex of diseases, each of which is treatable and preventable. This is truly the end of aging as we know it. We now believe that these diseases are partially the result of genetic coding expressed at the interface between the genes and the environment with the environment as a full partner in the aging process. The environment includes the food we eat, the nutritional supplements we take, our life styles and relationships.

Help Is On the Way

Geneticists are finally unraveling the genetic component of aging, and it is amazingly easy to understand. Chromo-

somes are the double-helixed, intertwined base pairs, which encode the instructions for the processes of life. These base pairs are incredibly long, numbering in the millions per chromosome and our species has 46 chromosomes. At the end of each chromosome is a string of base pairs—called telomeres (literally "tail pieces")—which do not code for anything, but rather serve to count the numbers of cell divisions. With each cell division an enzyme called telomerase is made which clips off the base pair from the end of the telomere. When the last base telomere is clipped off, the cell can no longer divide and the cell line dies of old age. Human cell lines can divide about 100 times before dying of old age.

The newest research in treating AIDS is the development of protease inhibitors. These are enzymes, which prevent the formation of protein by HIV cells when they try to replicate. A similar enzyme can be developed which would be called a telomerase inhibitor. This enzyme would prevent the clipping away of the telomeres and make human cell lines immortal.

In fact nature has already devised immortal human cell, the gonadal cell. These are the sperm and egg cells and they do not have a telomerase enzyme. Placed in cell culture, these cells divide indefinitely without aging! The solution to human aging will come when all cells in the body can be made immortal as the gonadal cells are already immortal. This development will come within 15-20 years according to conservative estimates of the best geneticists.

It will also be possible to rebuild the telomeres to their original length with enzymes designed for this job and it will also be possible to do genetic repair of the damage to chromosomes which has accumulated over the years. Brace yourself: what the geneticists are telling us is that not only can aging be halted, it can be reversed! We will be able to choose to grow young instead of grow old, to choose your favorite age, youth to that point and remain there. Dying will not be necessary![3]

Sometimes I am asked, "What happens if I invest long term and then get hit by a bus next Tuesday?" My answer is, "You've got no problem, other than the severe pain before you pass out. You enjoyed some extra income for the entire week and your spouse or heirs will enjoy higher income." If your beneficiaries don't want the longer-term security, they are free to sell it (note that fixed income investments sold prior to maturity may result in a profit or loss).

If you buy 15-year bonds and you last 15 years, then you have no problem. You only create problems for yourself if you buy short term investments that don't pay enough and you live a long time.

Think long term. You are probably going to be around longer than you think, so thinking long term will help you. As a passing note, my sociology professor in college said that the big difference between rich and poor people was that rich people think about the long term, while poor people focus on the short term.

Let's revisit the start of this last discussion. As people age, they tend to invest shorter and shorter term. I mentioned that this tendency satisfied a need for security. But what is the insecurity? What are people nervous about? When I asked this question to a group of seniors, this is how they responded:

---

[3] http://www.medical-library.net/sites/_aging_in_america.html

Advisor: *Why do seniors invest short term? What are they nervous about?*
Seniors: *Needing the money.*

Advisor: *Needing the money - for what?*
Seniors: *Food and rent...and emergencies.*

Advisor: *Emergencies - what type of emergencies?*
Seniors: *Medical.*

The nervousness is only about a particular type of medical issue. It's actually not about "routine" medical issues. Most people are covered by Medicare (if retired) and have coverage on top of that. They're either in an HMO or have a Medi-Gap policy. If they're working, they have medical coverage through their employer. So the nervousness is really about the next topic we need to address—long-term care.

2

LONG-TERM CARE

Most people know what Medicare says in matters of long-term care: "We're not paying." And neither will your health insurance.

Our health system is arranged to pay for acute care. By that I mean the kind of illness in which you get sick, spend a few days in the hospital, get treatment and then go home with some new medication. Our system is pretty good at treating people like cars:

- Bring it in for a diagnostic.
- We'll order and install any new parts.
- We'll recommend that you use better oil and get your filter changed every 8,000 miles.
- Come see us in 25,000 miles for a check-up.

But human beings don't work this way. Many of our illnesses are chronic, persist over long periods of time and may be incurable. Illnesses such as:

- Chronic Arthritis
- Parkinson's Disease
- Alzheimer's Disease
- Effects of Stroke
- Effects of Osteoporosis
- Multiple Sclerosis
- Lou Gehrig's Disease (ALS)

The biggest cost of these illnesses is not the few days individuals may spend in a hospital, it's the cost of care when they go home. Who will shop, clean, drive their car and take care of the routine activities of daily living if they can't walk? Medicare won't and neither will their health insurance. Some people are confused about this. They think that Medicare will pay for long-term care. Here are the facts about what Medicare will pay for:

- A person has been a hospital patient for three consecutive days, not counting the day of discharge.
- A person is admitted to the skilled nursing facility within 30 days of his/her hospital discharge.
- The services he/she requires is related to the condition for which he/she was treated in the hospital.
- They require skilled nursing services or rehabilitation services on a daily basis. (These services, as a practical matter, can only be provided on an inpatient basis.)
- His/her doctor orders and certifies at time of admission that he/she needs skilled care services on a daily basis, and again, certifies his/her need 14 days after admission and every 30 days thereafter.
- A Utilization Review Committee of professionals regularly reviews and approves their continued need for skilled care services.
- Their stay in the skilled nursing facility is 100 days or less.

There are three levels of nursing care: convalescent, intermediate and skilled. Only the sickest patients needing constant medical attention qualify for skilled care. It's the only kind of care that Medicare will subsidize for you. If you qualify for skilled care, Medicare pays for the first 20 days of skilled care. For days 21-100, it pays everything over the first $101.50 per day. Medicare pays nothing for treatment longer than 100 days.

Just this morning I was reading ***Modern Maturity Magazine*** from AARP. They talked about some drugs that look like they are helping with Alzheimer's. But, the article said, there are 4 million people in the United States that have Alzheimer's. In fact, about half of the people over age 85 in the U.S. are afflicted. Now, Medicare washes its hands of people like that. Sure, Medicare Part B pays for their medication, but not their care. Because Medicare says that it is an untreatable illness, then there's nothing they can do about it. So, there are a lot of people who have disabilities that Medicare says are not treatable illnesses. As a result, Medicare doesn't get involved and doesn't pay.

That's a shock to a lot of people who believe Medicare is their health safety net. The result is that we have millions of spouses who are tied to their residences and have to take care of their sick spouses or spend all kinds of money on home care or nursing home services.

What do many people do to prepare for such a disability? They keep money available in short-term investments for that contingency. This is not a good idea. It makes no sense to try and fund a catastrophic financial event by keeping some money hanging around in short-term investments at low rates. That's like keeping $500,000 in the bank to build a house in case yours burns down.

Nationally, the average cost of long term care is $138 per day.[4] At that rate, you can run through a lot of money very quickly. If someone stays in a long term care facility for four years, they are going to run through approximately $200,000. Remember, your chance of being afflicted by an illness that creates a need for long-term care is almost 50/50.[5]

---

[4] CNA Insurance 2001 market research figures, national average.
[5] Derived from 1997 National Nursing Home Survey, Society of Actuaries.

As you read in the last chapter, life expectancy continues to increase, which means we will have more people living longer and needing more years of care. You have three options to deal with the issue.

1. **Self fund.** Either keep $200,000 to $300,000 laying around or have sufficient income to come up with the additional $4000 to $6000 per month when the illness strikes. I know many people who can afford the cost and still get insurance protection because they'd rather leave their assets to their beneficiaries than consume them for long term care.

2. **Self-insure.** I know many people who have obtained long term care insurance to retain their independence. They do not want their beneficiaries making their health care decisions with assets from the general pool of their net worth. Sometimes family members can make less-than-optimal decisions when weighing how to spend their inheritance. Since funds from a long term care policy can only be used for long term care, it's a pot of money reserved solely for that use and cannot be derailed by family members or others.

3. **Go on Medicaid.** Medicaid is for people with few assets, although there are enough loopholes that anyone could qualify. For example, in many states, the primary residence is an "exempt" asset, which Medicaid cannot touch and which is not counted when determining Medicaid eligibility. That residence could be a 50-unit apartment building even though you only reside in one apartment. The entire building would be exempt. (Note: these rules and their implementation vary from state to state. Please check your state's rules at http://medicaid.aphsa.org/links.htm#states). However, you don't want to be on Medicaid. It's well docu-

mented that Medicaid patients get worse treatment than private pay patients in the medical community.[6] You lose your independence with Medicaid.

Get insurance. The long term care salesman will tell everybody, you need long term care insurance. Not true. If you've got enough assets, you could self fund. If you are poor, you can get Medicaid. So who needs insurance? It's the 80% of the people in the middle who need the insurance. So my caution to you is that you've got a substantial risk to your assets, which is this risk of long term care. And if you do not think that having the protection of insurance is important, then consider these few questions.

Table 2.1
Chances of Life Risk Occurrences and Insurance Coverage for Risks

Risks in Your Life	Chance of Occurrence	Are You Insured?
House Burning	1 in 240	yes
Car Crash	1 in 8	yes
Medical Problem	Yearly?	yes
Long Term Health Care	48 in 100	NO!

Sources for Table 2.1 include: ***2001***, National Safety Council; 3/31/00 ***National Fire Prevention Association***; and ***1997 Modification of National Nursing Home Survey***, Society of Actuaries.

[6] These two articles document this issue: ***Kiplinger's Retirement Report*** (www.kiplinger/retreport/archives/1999/August/living.htm) and ***National Senior Citizens Law Center Letter to Congressional Committee on Medicaid Discrimination*** (www.nsclc.org/mcaiddump.html).

Do you have car insurance? I'll bet you do. Do you have homeowner's insurance? I'll bet you have that, too. Your risk of your house burning is 1 in 240. The risk of being in a car accident is about 1 in 8.

You've got insurance for those risks though. The chance of your needing long term care if you're over 65 is almost five in ten. (About half of the cases of long term care continue for more than four months. Therefore, your chance of a prolonged illness is about one in four if you are over 65). Yet, you have no insurance. So why don't people insure knowing that the risk is this high, far higher than the risk of ruining your car or your house? Because it is too costly? Actually, your homeowner's insurance is also too costly. And so is your car insurance. After all, have you ever had the thought when paying an insurance bill, "I love paying this insurance, it's so affordable." It's all too costly isn't it?

(Reminds me of a father—he was trying to teach his son about money. The kid comes in and says, "Dad, lend me $50." The father exclaims, "$40! What do you need $30 for? Here's $20!")

What is really too costly is not to have the insurance. What's too costly is what it costs to pay the bill when you need to. What's too costly is when one spouse needs care and the other may be forced to decrease their standard of living to pay for it.

I would suggest to you that your homeowners insurance is far more costly than long term care protection. You've paid your homeowner's insurance all of your life, and the chances of you ever collecting on it are very tiny, because its very unlikely that your house will burn down or a plane smash into it. That's expensive insurance because you'll most likely never need it.

If your assets are low, you want to think about organizing your affairs to get government support. If you're in the middle, you need to think about getting insurance. It's as simple as that. Actually, the insurance isn't too expensive. I'll tell you why most people don't have long term care insurance. Most everyone has car insurance and homeowner's insurance. Most of what you learned about money, you learned from your parents. They had car insurance and homeowner's insurance, and now so do you. Did they have long-term care insurance? No, and now neither do you. We simply repeat what we have learned.

But this is a new era. Your parents did not need long-term care insurance. In fact, it did not exist. Why didn't it exist? People did not live as long 30 years ago. They got sick and died.

Figure 2.1
Chances of Needing Long Term Care

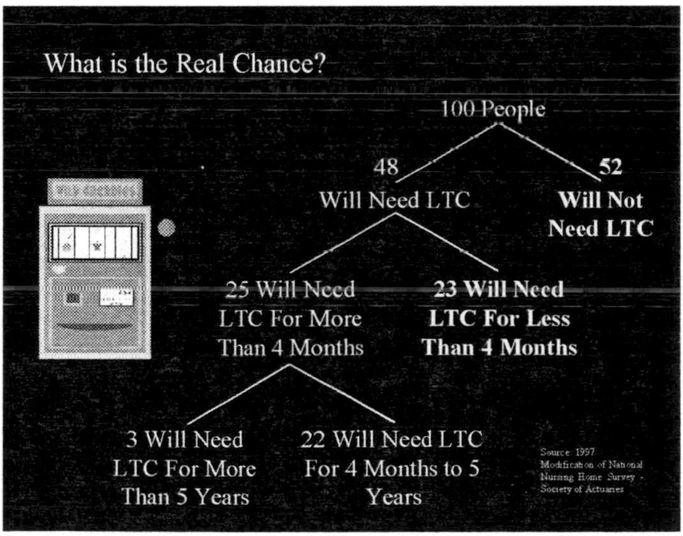

Congratulations! You are the first generation to need this type of protection. Your generation is the first one to live this long, requiring you to have this risk to your assets that previous generations didn't have. Your life span will outlive your body's ability to support it in comfort.

I predict those people who are in their forties now will all have long term care insurance by the time they reach 65. Why? Because they will have learned from their parents and observed the generation before them. I predict it will be built into the medical policy. Because, given what I showed you about life expectancies…how long will the average person live if he or she is 40 today? To the age of 90, 95 or 100?

Such life spans will be common. So, your generation is the transition generation. Your parents didn't need it. Your kids will certainly need it and you are right in the middle—the first group to live long enough to require long-term care protection. Now let's show you how to keep the cost of long term care insurance down.

The Return of Premium Rider

Would you like to get your money back if you do not use the insurance? Here's a hypothetical example of that: A 70-year-old takes out a very basic policy that would pay him $100 a day if he enters into a nursing home. In this hypothetical scenario, the policy pays $100 per day, for five years. The monthly premium is $95.

Now, by the way, this premium may seem low to you. I know it seems low because you've been talking to the long-term care salesman who wants to sell you the Rolls Royce policy. Have you ever noticed that a Chevrolet gets you to the same place just as well as a Rolls Royce? I'm going to show you the Chevrolet policy, because that will provide you basic protection. If you want more protection, I think that's great and I encourage you to get a policy with full benefits.

You can get basic coverage for $95 per month. Some companies offer to refund your premiums if you do not use the policy. In the example below, instead of $95 per month, you pay $95 plus $60 per month for this option. Assuming you keep the policy in force and have not used the benefits, all of the premiums paid are refunded at death, a total of $29,760 based on the average life expectancy of a 70-year-old male.

Table 2.2
Return of Premium Nursing Home Policy for a 70-Year-Old Male

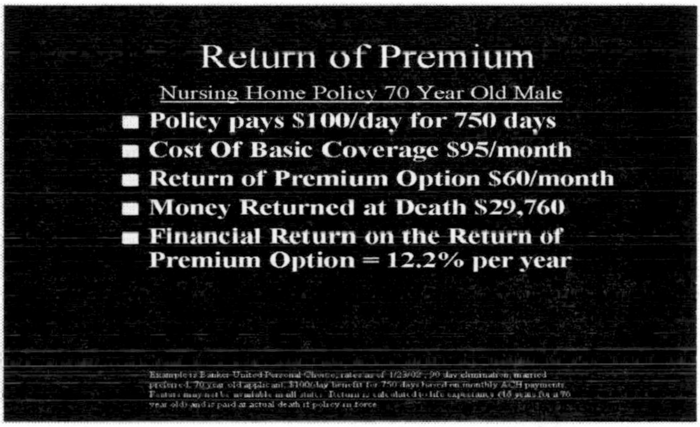

Return of Premium
Nursing Home Policy 70 Year Old Male
Policy pays $100/day for 750 days
Cost Of Basic Coverage $95/month
Return of Premium Option $60/month
Money Returned at Death $29,760
Financial Return on the Return of Premium Option = 12.2% per year

So, not a bad option to think about if you're the type of person thinking, "I'd like this protection, but I don't think I'm ever gonna need it." With insurance, you have to get it when you don't need it. Did you ever notice that the insurance company won't sell you fire insurance while your house is burning down? (About 8 years ago I had a woman come see me. She asked about getting long term care insurance. I gave her the information she requested, then she came back two weeks later and said, "My doctor says I don't need it!")

The insurance companies only want your business when you don't need the insurance, because when you need it, they aren't selling. With the return of premium option, you can get the insurance when you're healthy and your family can recover all of the premiums at death if you don't use the insurance.

Single Pay, Premium Recovery

Many people would obtain this insurance if they did not need to make annual payments. There are a few companies that have designed their policies so that individuals don't have to keep paying them money every year. Instead, they pay one premium and they are done. The best part is that they can always get the premium back!

The policy acts like a savings account (with life insurance included) and the interest from your one-time single premium is used to pay the annual long term care premium. Consider the following hypothetical example.

A 70-year-old deposits a $50,000 premium. The policyholder recovers his/her money back in one of three ways.

1. They keep the policy indefinitely. In which case their beneficiaries receive $74,000 when they die. There's life insurance included in the policy.

2. They'll need nursing care, so the policy pays for that—up to $148,000. They'll have that much available if they need it for long term care.

3. They cancel the policy some time in the future. They have their $50,000 earning interest and it will just grow like a savings account. If they want to close it out, then they can close it out.

Figure 2.2
Single Pay Premium Recovery Option for a 70-Year-Old Person

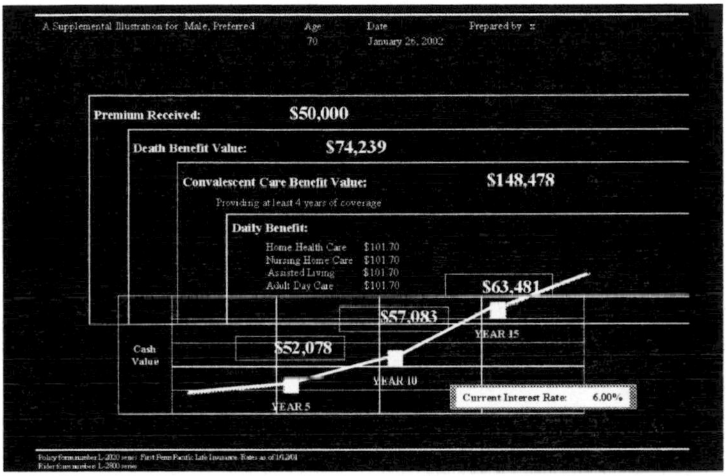

So, this was the insurance industry's answer to people who said, "I don't want to pay premiums and not get anything back." Here, they invite people to deposit $50,000 with them and they'll always get back more than they put in. Either their kids will get it, they'll get it through collecting on the long term care insurance or they'll take out the deposit with interest.

There are other ways to get this protection without it costing a lot of money. Let's take a look at some other money-saving ideas:

Immediate Annuity Option

Similar to the above scenario, a person makes a single premium payment. Immediately, they receive a payment each year that they can use to pay their long term care premium. Here's a hypothetical example:

A 70-year-old male makes a $20,000 single premium payment for an immediate annuity. He receives $2000 a year for life from the annuity (*Annuity Shopper*, 4/5/02). He uses this payment to make annual payments for his long-term care policy. At the end of his life, the annual payments stop and he does not get back any of his $20,000. This plan is unlike the above example, which requires a larger single payment but returns the payment in any of the three scenarios reviewed. (Please see the chapter on annuities for a more complete discussion of annuities.)

When Should You Get Insurance?

You should obtain insurance as early as possible. The longer you wait, the more expensive it gets. In general, each year you wait to start a policy, the premium jumps about 10%. Some people ask me if they would be better off saving money to prepare for a long-term care situation instead of investing in insurance. The problem is that you could never save enough to equal what an insurance policy would pay.

Let's say that at age 50, you started saving $680 per year for your future long-term care needs. Invested at 12% annually, you would accumulate $164,000 over 30 years. But in 30 years, the cost of four years in a nursing home could be well over $600,000! You can never accumulate enough through saving $680 per year. However, the same amount invested in long-term care insurance would provide a policy with benefits of $631,000 to help handle the cost (this example is based on a major insurance company's comprehensive policy rates with four years of coverage, a 90-day elimination period, preferred health rating and an initial daily benefit of $100 per day with 5% compounded inflation).

It is also a good idea to start a policy early because the premiums are lower. But most importantly, it's a good idea to start early so you can qualify for coverage. As you age and the risk of adverse medical conditions becomes greater, you run the risk of not qualifying for insurance. We see many people who wait so long that they develop medical conditions and notations in their medical records that make them uninsurable.

Does this mean if you're already 78 years old that you cannot get insurance? Not at all. The insurance companies do accept many pre-existing medical conditions and there is no cost to apply. So certainly apply if you want this protection, but do it now, rather than later.

Two Important Reasons to Get Long-Term Care Insurance

This insurance is for your spouse and your children. If you get sick and need help, who do you think will bear the burden? If you're married, you will turn your spouse's life upside down, from an easy retirement into a dreary existence. Is that what you want? If you're single, your kids will pay. They will either feel obligated to help you and make arrangements to fit you into their already over worked schedules or they will probably resent it (although they would never say so). If you don't get long-term care insurance you can also deplete your assets—money that would otherwise have gone to your children. Therefore, it's important to realize that a major reason to purchase long term care insurance is to protect your family.

The other reason is to preserve your independence. Do you want your children helping you brush your teeth? Do you want family members deciding how to spend your assets for your care? Insurance provides a separate pot of money that can be used only for your quality care. You can use it to get quality care from professionals, whether inside or outside your home. You keep your independence.

What Does Long-Term Care Insurance Cost?

The cost can vary widely depending on the company you choose and the coverage you select. For example, one company may charge a lot for inflation protection. While another may have a lower charge for inflation, but they may charge more for home care. I have analyzed coverage for hundreds of seniors and there is no single company that is the lowest cost in all cases.

Therefore, the first step is to decide on the coverage you want, then your advisor can get quotes from several companies and find the best quotation for the coverage you desire. Here are some recommendations. There are four important items to consider when choosing coverage.

1. **Inflation Protection.** This protection will increase your insurance benefit over time to hopefully keep pace with the actual cost of long-term care. If you are under age 75, definitely purchase the inflation coverage because hopefully it will be many years until you need the benefits. However, when you do need the coverage, the cost will be a lot higher and you'll be glad that you have the inflation-adjusted benefit.

2. **Benefit Period.** You select how much coverage you want. I recommend that people apply for four years or more. The coverage period determines how many years the insurance company will pay your benefits once you need them. Only 6% of the people who need nursing care need it for five years or more. Therefore, if you obtain coverage for at least four years, you have enough coverage to cover 94% of long term care incidences. If you are worried about needing more coverage, you can get longer coverage, up to a lifetime.

3. **Daily Benefit.** This is how much the insurance company will pay you per day. I recommend at least $100 per day coverage. That gives you $3000 per month. So if your actual cost were $4000, between the insurance and your Social Security income, you could probably cover the total cost.

4. **Coverage for In-the-Home and Outside-the-Home.** You can select where you want to be covered. While many people like the idea of remaining in their own home and desire insurance for in-the-home care, the more important insurance is for outside of the home (e.g., nursing home or assisted living facility). There are two reasons for this.

   (A) In your own home, the care you need is usually more moderate (homemaker duties such as shopping, cooking, cleaning, bill paying) and the cost is less. Often friends, neighbors and family can lend a hand. It's much easier, financially, to cover in-home care costs. If you do need to go outside the home, the cost is large and that's when you really need the insurance.

   (B) Your home may be a bad place for you if you're ill. Stairs, long distances to the car and narrow doorways can all present problems for people with walkers or wheelchairs. Often, it's easiest and more sensible to obtain care outside the home.

I'm not dissuading you from getting insured for in-home care, I just want you to know which type of long-term care insurance is more important. Get both coverages if your budget allows for that, but otherwise, (at the minimum) get insurance for outside-the-home care.

Six Ways to Reduce the Cost of Long-Term Care Insurance

You may find that long-term care salespeople want to sell you the most expensive policy. While I believe that you should have complete coverage (inflation protection, lifetime coverage, at least $100/day benefit), it is better to have at least a basic policy than to have none at all. In other words, a minimum policy is better than being uncovered for the high cost of long term care. In order to help you minimize the cost of insurance, I have compiled a list of six ways to help you reduce costs and ensure that you have basic coverage. None of us know when a health catastrophe will strike. Heart attack, stroke, cancer, Parkinson's and Alzheimer's are all debilitating illnesses which give no advance warning. Protect yourself and your family financially.

Here are six ways to get covered at a lower cost:

1. **Reduce the coverage period.** For example, reduce the term of the policy from four years to three years. Savings can still be significant and a three-year policy covers 80% of the cases of long term care.

2. **Reduce the daily benefit.** The actual cost of nursing care averages $138/day. If you cover just $100 or $90 per day with insurance, many people can make up the difference with social security or interest income.

3. **If you are age 75 or over, consider dropping the inflation protection.** Although you will hopefully never need long term care, if you do, you are likely to need it within ten years—by age 85. Therefore, you do not need to protect for inflation over as long a period of time as, for example, a 65-year-old.

4. **Consider partial home care coverage.** Many companies offer, as an example, $100/day benefit for nursing home payments and $50/day for home care payments (home care payments are typically less expensive). By reducing the benefits for home care you can lower your premium.

5. **Eliminate home care insurance.** Many people have a spouse or friends and relatives who can assist them in the home. Hired home aides are relatively inexpensive ($12-$18 per hour). Care at home may easily be covered within the means of your own income. The most important coverage to obtain is for care outside of the home.

6. **Consider the return of premium option.** Although this makes the monthly premium more expensive, some or all (depending on the company) of the premiums you pay will be refunded to you if you do not use the insurance. This makes the overall cost of insurance very inexpensive for those fortunate people who do not incur long term care expenses.

3

Mutual Funds

Beware of Last Year's Best Funds

Have you ever seen those mutual fund advertisements with mouth-watering returns of 40% or 50% in the last 12 months? You decide to invest some of your sluggish funds and jump into these "winners." And then, as soon as you get in, these "winners" turn to losers and start declining in value. Do you ever feel that you might be financially jinxed? That as soon as *you* get into an investment, it declines?

Don't worry, others have had the same experience. This losing experience results from the way mutual funds advertise their results, investors' behaviors and the "tendency toward the mean." First, let's look at the advertisements. When do you think a mutual fund company decides to advertise a specific fund—just after a losing period or a winning period? Of course, they advertise a fund just after it has had a great return (and sometimes, just as it's about to cool off). You can, therefore, avoid such situations by ignoring mutual fund advertisements. These hot funds or "star" funds historically do very poorly after their best period, as the following two studies show.

As Eric Tyson, financial columnist, summarized in 1997, "Over the subsequent 3, 5 and 10-year periods, a whopping 80 percent of these 'star' funds performed worse than the average similar fund." The "star" funds were those funds ranked #1 in their category the previous year.[7] (See Appendix A for a copy of Eric Tyson's *"Star Funds Often Burn Out Quickly"* article).

In fact, the least popular fund categories have done better than the best performing fund categories as reported in an annual Morningstar Study.[8] Since 1987, the least popular funds have outperformed 90% of the most popular funds over the following three years.

A related problem is investor behavior. Many investors will jump into a fund just after a fund advertises a very good period. Then, once investors are on board, the fund performance weakens. This often happens when a fund is new and small. At the beginning, the fund is maneuverable and may show a good track record. (Because of its small size, it is able to invest in smaller, potentially rapidly growing companies without owning an excessive amount of a small company's stock.) Then investors pile in, attracted by the good results, and the fund loses its maneuverability. With its increased size, the fund is forced to invest more money as it pours in and must naturally reduce its choices of investment candidates (i.e., it must seek out large companies in which to invest its larger sums). As pointed out in the Eric Tyson study and ***Money Magazine***,[9] this "hot streak" phenomenon is often followed by a steep decline in the fund's performance.

Who is to blame? The investors themselves—for chasing hot performance numbers, for bailing out at the first sign of trouble and for ignoring how important their own behavior is in determining how much they will make in mutual funds.

[7] *"Star Funds Burn Out Quickly,"* by Eric Tyson, ***San Francisco Chronicle***, March 8, 1997.
[8] Morningstar Principia Pro Commentary, "Buying Unloved Funds" 2/21/01.
[9] *"Funds That Really Make Money for Their Investors,"* ***Money Magazine***, April 1997, p. 124.

The third problem is a statistical phenomenon called "regression toward the mean." As it applies to mutual funds, it means that mutual fund categories will all perform about the same over the long term. Some categories will do well for a period of time, beat the market and then do poorly over the next several years and underperform the market. Conversely, those fund categories that did poorly before start doing better. So over the really long run, all funds perform about the same.[10]

For example, biotechnology funds will do well for a while and beat the market. Then, they will have a period of terrible performance. You can observe the same cycle for most any fund category, such as Pacific Rim Funds (great in the early 90s, terrible in the late 90s), REITs (poor performance in the 80s, much better in the 90s) and precious metal funds (significant performance in the 70s and 80s, terrible performance in the 90s). Over the long term, these categories all converge toward the average market return.

So be careful about chasing the advertised funds, since today's winner can be tomorrow's dog. Your best defense may be an "all weather" strategy. This strategy eliminates the need to jump in and out of hot categories and guess which funds are the "best" right now. An all-weather strategy puts you in funds that are right for you and are changed when your situation changes, not when a particular fund category looks "hot."

Selecting Funds

From 1991 through 2001, 72% of domestic equity mutual

---

[10] Sir Francis Galton published a paper entitled, "Regression Towards Mediocrity in Hereditary Stature," in 1885. This concept has been applied many times to describe investment performance.

funds performed worse than the S&P 500.[11] So during the period discussed in Figure 3.1, the odds were stacked against people beating the market with mutual funds. That's why selecting the right funds is critical.

Figure 3.1
Percentage of Domestic Equity Funds That Beat the S&P 500

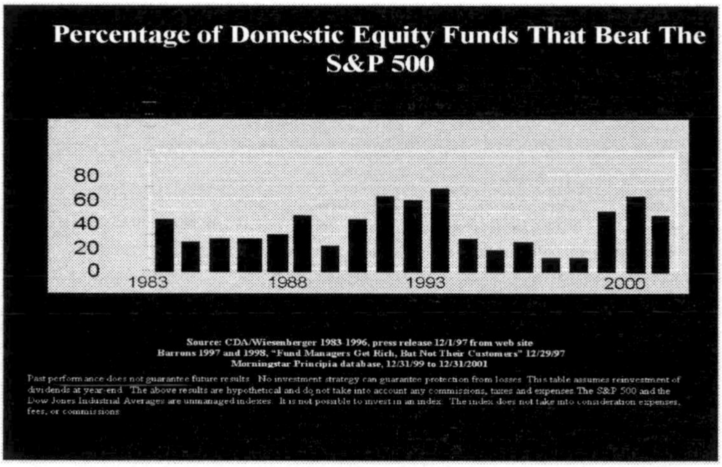

The problem is, no one knows how to select the fund that will appreciate a lot in advance. You can, however, select funds with reasonable costs and the appropriate risk profile. I have observed that many investors seem satisfied with their portfolios when the funds are selected at a comfortable risk level rather than when they attempt to capture big gains. Let's take a closer look:

There are many ways to measure risk, but for most investors, the real-world question looms, "How much could I lose?" But even this question is not a good one. Equity mutual funds by nature hold a basket of stocks. Let's assume for our example—100 stocks. Even if five of the companies comprising 5% of the value of the fund went

---

[11] The S&P 500 is an unmanaged index which cannot be invested in directly, based on comparison of S&P 500 index return and domestic equity funds ranked by Morningstar.

completely bankrupt and shut their doors, the fund would drop 5%, assuming everything else is unchanged; but rarely do companies go completely bankrupt. Therefore, the question about risk should not be about permanent loss since permanent loss situations are rare.

The more appropriate question is how much temporary loss can you tolerate? Even during the Depression, many losses were temporary, not permanent. AT&T, GM, Alcoa and many other companies survived, but their stock prices sure went down for a number of years, creating a temporary loss for investors. Those investors who held on experienced the loss on paper only.

Therefore, one way to select funds that meet your risk profile is to look at how they performed during a period of significant decline such as 1973/1974 or 1987. Although there is no assurance that past behavior guarantees future performance, there is some evidence that past risk has been a good predictor of future risk.

A Morningstar study looked at five years of fund data and also found that past performance was a very unreliable predictor of future performance. However, "the connection between past risk and future risk was very powerful…the riskiest funds stayed the riskiest and the safest stayed the safest."[12] In other words, the data suggests that selecting funds by risk level is a lot more reliable and that when measuring risk, past risk did predict future risk (the finding may be different for other periods that were not tested).

Herein lies a secret. Many investors select funds focused on past return. However, the more reliable indictor of the future is risk. A wise investor will manage their risk, because they have no control over the returns anyway! Talk to a truly professional investor and they will tell you that the number one issue they attend to is risk management. Profes-

[12] *"Putting Risk in Its Place,"* by John Rekenthaler, Morningstar editorial 5/27/94. In the study, risk was defined as standard deviation.

sionals do not guess at returns or make forecasts; they plot the probabilities, which means they seek to get the biggest return for the least risk. It's the risk they can control. You actually know this intuitively if you've ever been in a casino. You can sit at the $10 table or the $100 table. If you selected the $10 table, you are managing your risk. It's a smart way to deal with money.

Limit Your Fees

Below is a Morningstar Report, which gives you an overview of a mutual fund. I crossed out the name of the fund, but it's a great example of where to look for the fees.

Figure 3.2
Sample Mutual Fund Expenses

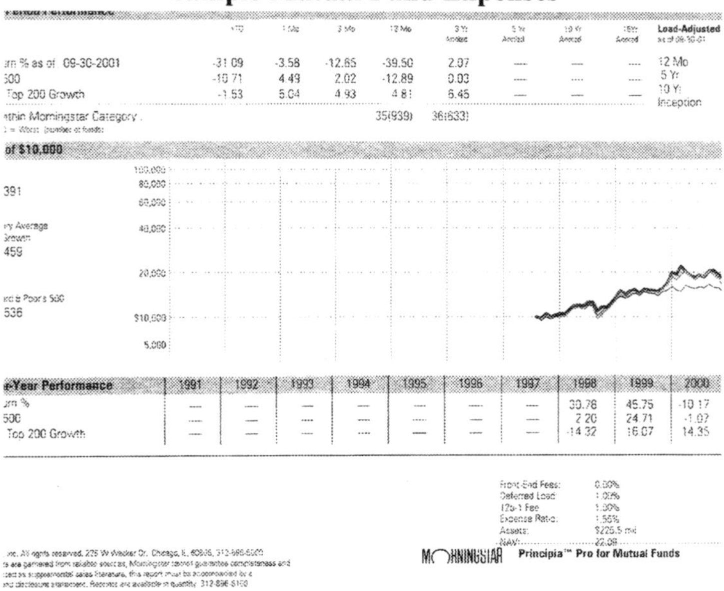

Reprinted with permission of Morningstar, Inc.

Chicago-based Morningstar, Inc. is a leading provider of investment information, research, and analysis. Its extensive line of Internet, software, and print products provides unbiased data and commentary on mutual funds, U.S. and international equities, closed-end funds, and variable annuities. Established in 1984, Morningstar continues to be the industry's most trusted source on key investment issues of the day. For more information about Morningstar, visit www.morningstar.com or call 800-735-0700.

When you buy a fund there are three types of expenses. First, there is the *management fee*. This expense covers the cost of creating a nice report for the fund... you know it's full color and it tells you how great the fund has been doing. You pay for the fund manager, all the researchers, the postage and the lawyers. That comes out of the balance of your fund. So, for the above fund, the management fee totals .58% of the money.

Now, this particular fund is sold through a securities firm and is a "B" share. In my experience, a few brokers misrepresent these shares. I have heard some brokers explain to their clients that there is no up-front load with "B" shares, which is true. They tell you that if you keep it for five years, then you can redeem the shares and have no cost to redeem. That's also true. What they may not mention, is that instead of an up-front load, there is an annual charge that is taken from your account—what the industry calls a *12b-1 fee*, which is usually 1% and is taken out of your balance. So instead of paying 5% commission up front, you pay 1% a year. So the 12b-1 fee is the second fee. Now you have a total of 1.58% annually in fees from these two costs.[13]

Now, there is a third cost that most people forget about. The mutual fund buys and sells stocks during the year, however, it doesn't do that for free. As a matter of fact, it's very expensive. It costs more for a mutual fund to transact the buy or sell than it does for you. You might think that it's large, so it must be cheaper for the mutual fund to trade. Right? Well, it's *because* the mutual fund is so large that there's a problem. Not only does a mutual fund pay commission (typically only one to two cents per share), but the fund incurs a *slippage cost*.

---

[13]Mutual fund shares are also offered as A shares and C shares. A shares have a front load but a smaller or no 12b-1 fee. At most fund companies, b shares convert to A shares after 6 to 8 years to reduce the 12b-1 fee. C shares are sold without a front load but have a continuing 12b-1 fee.

What do you think happens to the price of stock XYZ when the fund buys one million shares of stock? The buying pushes up the price of stock. Hypothetically, if the shares are selling today for $60 each, I can go buy my 500 shares or 200 shares at $60 because my 200 or 500 shares don't matter. What do you think happens when the fund comes to the market with an order for a million shares? The fund doesn't get them at $60. It hypothetically gets the first few at $60...the next few at $60.50...the next few at $61...and so on.

How much do these "market impact costs" affect the investor? Market impact cost is not something you find in a fund's financial statement. But it can be detected through analysis of the trading records. The cost to shareholders can be high—1% to 5% a year, depending on the size and liquidity of the stocks that a fund trades and the style of trading. "Funds that invest in small-cap stocks have higher impact costs than those that buy large-caps," says Nicolo Torre, a managing director at BARRA Inc., an investment consulting firm. And funds that practice a momentum strategy—buying what's hot—usually end up paying more than value investors that buy and hold. The only way to cut market impact costs, Torre says, is through fewer trades. "Ten percent of the trades reflect 90% of the market impact cost. Halve the number of trades, and you can significantly lower the fund's market impact cost."[14]

Here's another comment by an industry insider: John Bogle, ex-chairman of the Vanguard funds quotes a study in the ***Financial Analysts Journal***. Here's what he quotes… "A 1993 study in the ***Financial Analysts Journal*** suggested the cost of an average transaction was equivalent to 6/10 of 1%."[15] What does that mean? The fund discussed above had a turnover ratio of 256%. That particular mutual fund

[14] *"Mutual Funds: What's Wrong?"* ***Business Online***, 01/24/00.
[15] ***Bogle on Mutual Funds*** by John Bogle, Dell, 1994.

changed its stocks 2.5 times during the year. So the stocks the fund had on January 1st were sold, then the fund bought new ones and sold those, then the fund bought new ones and sold half again. So 2.5 times, which is actually at total of five transactions. Mr. Bogle is saying that for each transaction it costs the fund 6/10 of a percent. So now there is 3% incurred for the true cost of buying and selling (5 times 0.6%).

By the way—you will never see this cost of turnover quantified in any prospectus. The prospectus will only show the turnover figure, but not the cost of the slippage. Most people who work at mutual funds don't even understand it. Call your fund company and ask them the cost of slippage or market impact costs and they won't know what you are asking. So, if I add all of the costs together—the management fee, the 12b-1 fee and the slippage cost—you have a total cost of owning the fund at 4.58%. Granted, it's on the high side, but out of your money each year, it costs you about 4.58% per year to have shares in that fund.

Why do I show you this? Because many investors are not aware. Some years ago I had a woman ask me how much I charge to manage portfolios. I explained the cost and she said, "That's too high, I don't pay anything in my mutual fund!"

Taxes

When you buy individual stocks, you get built-in tax deferral. You pay no capital gains tax until you sell your shares. Not so with a mutual fund. Every time the fund sells a stock for a profit, you must pay tax on your share of the profit, even if you have not received any distribution. The gain incurred by the fund may be a long-term capital gain (taxed at federal rates up to 20%) or the fund may have short-term capital gains (taxed at up to 38.6%). Each year you receive a

1099 form to disclose on your tax return and you pay taxes on these gains (in addition to the dividends).

Here's the worst irritation—these taxes are even higher in years when the market falls and fund investors create net redemptions in the fund. When more fund shareholders want to sell rather than buy (which usually happens when the market is falling and investors get scared), the fund will sell its holdings in order to create cash to pay the selling shareholders. These sales by the fund of its stocks often create capital gains and these will be reflected on your 1099. So in years when you watch your fund decline in value, you may also get the biggest tax bill!

Here's an option. Many fund managers also manage sub-accounts within variable annuities. In many cases, these sub-accounts are almost identical to the mutual fund managed by that same fund manager and reflect the fund manager's style. The great aspect of variable annuities is that you do not receive an annual 1099. Rather, when you liquidate portions of your variable annuity, you will pay tax on the gain at ordinary income rates (up to 38.6%).[16]

---

[16] There is also a tax benefit exclusive to annuities when they are annuitized. Of each payment, the IRS considers a part of your periodic payments return of your original investment, which is not taxed and part is your gain, which is taxed at ordinary rates. Note that withdrawals prior to age 59½ are subject to a 10% penalty. This is not a comprehensive discussion of tax issues and you should consult a tax advisor. Variable annuities are issued by insurance companies, whereby investors can choose among various investment sub-accounts. Similar to mutual funds, these sub-accounts are professionally managed diversified portfolios, which may offer less risk than individual stocks and bonds and contain continuing fees and charges. In addition to the charges in the sub-accounts, there may be additional mortality charges and expenses. Income taxes on variable annuities are deferred. Withdrawals prior to age 59½ are subject to a 10% penalty.

So there is a tradeoff of avoiding taxes each year yet potentially paying a higher tax later. Additionally, variable annuities provide a death benefit, which carries a cost. The only way to determine if a variable annuity would offer a savings for you is to run an analysis for your personal tax situation. I am happy to provide such an analysis at no charge.

Turnover

The turnover rate in a fund is not necessarily a bad thing, but as mentioned, it does increase your tax bill if the fund is selling stocks with a great deal of short-term gains. Additionally, as mentioned in the previous section on cost, turnovers cost you money. If turnover does hurt a fund's return, wouldn't there be a correlation between a fund's turnover rate and its after-tax return? Indeed there is!

As reported by Morningstar on August 15, 1997 in *"The Low Turnover Advantage,"* the lower a fund's turnover, the higher its returns, in general. Over a ten-year period ending 6/30/97, Morningstar found that low turnover funds (under 20% turnover) beat high turnover funds (turnover over 100%) by an average of 1.58% annually. The exception was in small-cap funds, where high turnover funds did better.

The conclusion of the study: "Although our study admittedly covers a limited time period, it makes a strong case that for many domestic-stock categories, less-active managers are more successful. Investors are particularly unlikely to benefit from high-turnover strategies among large-cap value and blended funds and the rewards of turnover are also fairly small for most other categories." Please note that this study only analyzed the effect that turnover has on performance. High turnover also increases the investor's tax impact.

Derivatives and Style Drift

Do you know that your fund might borrow money to buy securities? Are you comfortable knowing that your fund might borrow money (in an effort to buy more stocks and enjoy gains) which could magnify losses if the market falls? Do you know if your fund uses volatile derivatives in order to boost returns? Derivatives are financial instruments, whose up and down price movements are based on the movements of an underlying security, such as a stock or bond. However, the derivative's volatility is much greater. If the stock moves 10% in value, the derivative could move 50%.

These issues are mentioned in your fund's prospectus, but you will not know that your fund is using these tactics until after the fact (when you get the semi-annual report). Some funds have created significant losses through the use of derivatives and fortunately, the fund management companies reimbursed the fund shareholders for their errors. As stated in ***Barron's*** on August 23, 1999, "Five years ago, bad derivative bets nearly undid a number of funds, but investors were bailed out in those cases as well."

Included in this topic is the issue of style drift. For example, you might invest in a value fund, which focuses on large "blue chip" companies selling at modest price earnings ratios. But the fund manager may get tempted by the fast increase in Internet stocks and start allocating the fund's money into these investments. Is that what you thought you were getting? According to a recent study by the Association for Investment Management, nearly 40% of all mutual funds are classified inaccurately based on stated goals versus actual investment and management.

You can avoid this problem of style drift by using funds that can never vary from their stated style in their prospectus. You can read an excellent article on funds that avoid this problem at *www.brill.com/expert/expls11001.html.*

Putting Together a Mutual Fund Portfolio

Assembling a fund portfolio is not done by selecting a bunch of funds that seem to have done well lately. But that's exactly what many investors do. Based on the last six months of ***Money Magazine*** or whatever publication they prefer, investors buy the funds highlighted in the editorial stories.

The problem is, if those funds have all been rising together, they will most likely all fall together. The goal should be selecting funds that are complementary, so that your overall return will be a smooth, rather than a concentrated boom or bust pattern resembling a roller coaster ride. (Note that there is no allocation or system to assemble a portfolio that will assure a profit.)

4

INVESTING IN STOCKS

How can you make money in the stock market? Whether you use mutual funds or individual stocks, you need to understand how the market works. I'll show you how it works in ten minutes.

Now, there was a time, I should mention, when I didn't have a clue about the stock market. I was in college and there was a guy who lived in my dormitory—a real smart guy. He never went to class, but he got all A's. He had those real thick glasses, you know, a real smart guy. He stayed in his room all of the time. He had charts of these stocks all over the wall and he had two computers. There was no computer store in those days, so you had to mail away for a computer and when it came, you built it. So he's in there with his computers; he's not going to class; he's got these charts.

I ignored him most of college and then, when I was a senior, I thought, "You know, I need to get serious here. I need to make some money. What am I going to do?" So I go down and I talk to Ed. I say, "Ed, clearly you know everything about the stock market. What do I need to know to end up with one million dollars in the stock market in the next five years?" He pulls down his glasses and looks squarely at me over the top of the frames and he says, "Start with two million dollars."

Let me show you how the stock market really works. These are facts. I'm not giving you my opinions about this. The facts are worth quite a bit. Figure 4.1 shows what happened if you invested in stocks and held them for a year. It also shows what has happened since 1926. It shows that if you had invested in the S&P 500, had bought some stocks and had held onto them for a year, then you would have made money 71% of the time. What happened the other 29% of the time? You lost money.

Figure 4.1
S&P 500 One Year Holding Periods

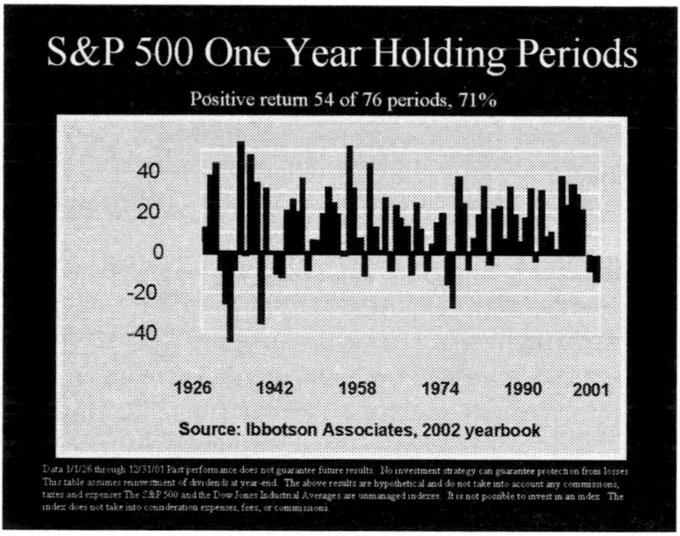

That's not a very winning percentage as far as I'm concerned. It's not good enough. On the following page there's another figure that looks similar, but shows something a little different. If you had bought stocks and held them for five years, then what was your chance of making money? Based on history, your chance would have been 90%.

Figure 4.2
S&P 500 Five Year Holding Periods

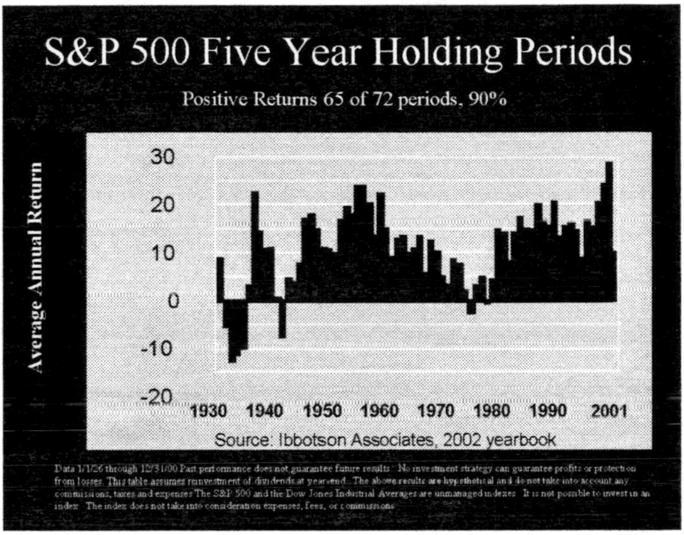

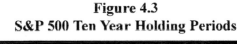

What happened if you had bought stock and held them ten years? Now I'm starting to get interested. Based on history, your chance of profit would have been 97%.

Figure 4.3
S&P 500 Ten Year Holding Periods

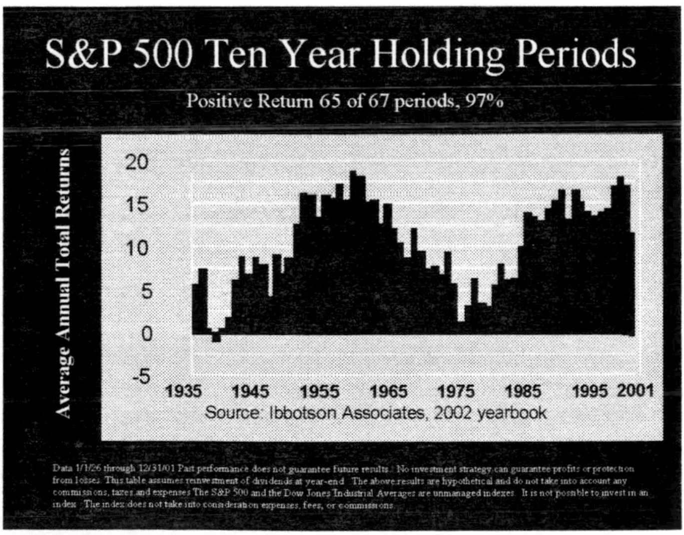

Since 1926 if you bought some stocks and held them 15 years, then what was the percentage of time you'd make money? Always. (Remember, these are historical figures and past performance is not a guarantee of success).

Figure 4.4
S&P 500 Fifteen Year Holding Periods

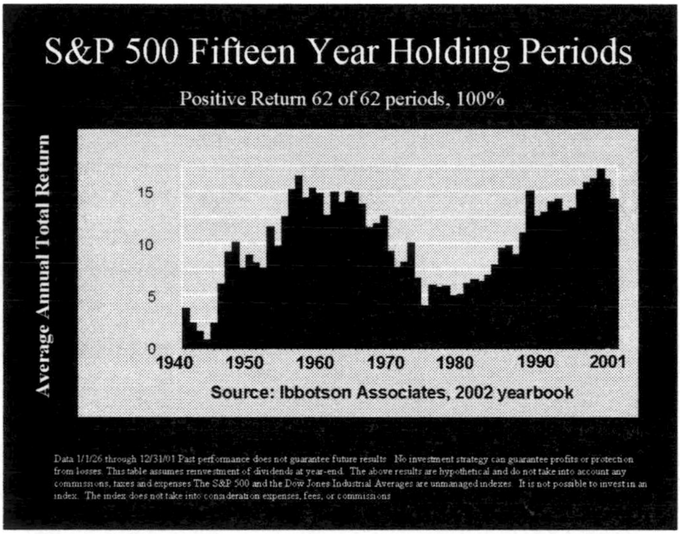

What do the four charts tell us about the stock market? You have to have a long-term time horizon. It's a very simple concept, but it's unbelievable how many people are worried about what the stock market's gonna do this year or today!

The way people act impatiently about the stock market reminds me of little children. If you have ever been with children after their mother has left on an errand, they usually ask something like, "When's my mom coming back?" You answer, "In about an hour." Five minutes later they say,

"Has it been an hour yet?" That's how adults act with stocks.

You can see from these charts that patience has increased the probability of investing success tremendously. Yet people keep watching CNBC everyday and reading the business section and investment newsletters as if they will learn anything that will help them. The thing you can learn right here is be patient!

People say to me, "What's the stock market gonna do this year?" It's an incredibly foolish question. But I will give you the most accurate answer. Based on history since 1926, the market has a 71% chance of rising this calendar year. Any other answer is full of conjecture, speculation and an opinion that won't buy you a cup of coffee.

You cannot invest expecting to have good results by listening to news reports. The daily news is inconsequential. This is what confuses people about the stock market. You'll hear on the news that the economy is doing wonderfully. They will come out with a positive unemployment report stating that more people have jobs and there's less unemployment, yet the stock market will go down 100 points that day. And it makes no sense to you.

You'll say wait, if the economy is doing good, then why is the stock market going down? I will explain that very simply. The stock market knows nothing about short term. You're looking at one day and you want to make sense out of it. Can't do it. Won't work. You need to look at it in big chunks of time and then it makes perfect sense. What has the stock market done over time? How has it fared over the last 10, 20 or 30 years? It's gone up. And what has happened to the U.S. economy? It's grown. Now it all makes perfect sense doesn't it?

Peter Lynch, the legendary fund manager who guided

the Magellan fund for an annualized return of 23% over 15 years, said it again and again. He said stock prices move in tandem with long-term earnings. When you look at it over the right time frame, it will all make perfect sense. There is no confusion about it. So, please don't ask how will the market do this year. I don't know. Nobody does. I promise you, nobody does. Peter Lynch, a very smart guy, provides perspective on the market. He says in his book, ***One Up on Wall Street***, "This taught me that it's not only difficult to predict the market, but also that the small investors tend to be pessimistic and optimistic at precisely the wrong time so it's self defeating to try and invest in good markets and get out of bad ones."[17]

In other words, he's saying, "Don't worry about it. You're not going to get it right anyway." As for himself, he says, "Obviously you don't have to be able to predict the stock market to make money in stocks or else I wouldn't have made any money." He concludes that if you ask him where the market is going, he is going to answer that he doesn't have a clue. So, please don't ask that question.

Invest for ten years and you'll increase the probability of success substantially, based on historical data. And if you think ten years is too long, then the only thing I have to tell you is that you better be investing for as long as you'll be around. So, ten years for most people is probably not too long, it's probably too short.

In addition to patience, you need an investing system. By system I mean some method that takes your emotions out of the equation. Whether you realize it or not, or like it or not, your emotions are the things that make you lose money in the market. The market never makes you lose money. The market just keeps doing its thing. It's only the fact that

[17] ***One Up On Wall Street*** by Peter Lynch, Penguin Books, NY, p. 30.

you get nervous and sell or buy at the wrong time that's to blame for the situations you find yourself in.

Most people read the newspaper. They read stuff like this on the front page of the business section: **"Dow Plunges 2.3%, Rates Rise Sharply."**[18] Do you know how many people sold stocks that day? That headline made them nervous and many people think that what's in the newspaper is important. Six weeks later, the same newspaper screamed on the front page of the business section: **"Dow Soars 143 to Record High."**[19] On that day you would have decided you better buy. So if you want to know when the market will turn a corner according to the newspaper, just wait six weeks. If you are serious about investing, please don't read the financial section of the newspaper. (See Appendix B for copies of the two articles that accompany the headlines featured above).

Read the financial news and consider it all as a comic strip. This stuff will play with your emotions and make you think incorrectly about investing. You will be instigated to make short-term changes rather than be a long-term investor. You read the news and then it seeps into your brain and it sits there for a day. When you hear another negative or positive economic item or a third one, then you start thinking, "I better buy or I better sell." It's all emotion driven. You've got to get that out of the way if you want to potentially make money in the market.

Terry Odean is a Professor at the University of California at Davis. He studies investor behavior. Here's what he has found about human emotions and investing. He discovered that the particular group of people he studied sold securities that did better than the securities they bought.

"This paper takes a first step towards demonstrat-

[18] March 14, 1997, ***San Francisco Chronicle***.
[19] May 6, 1997, ***San Francisco Chronicle.***

ing that overall trading volume in equity markets is excessive, by showing that it is excessive for a particular group of investors: those with discount brokerage accounts. One possible cause of excessive trading is overconfidence. Overconfident investors will trade too frequently, that is, the gains overconfident investors realize through trade will be less than they anticipate and may not even offset trading costs."

"By analyzing trading records for 10,000 accounts at a large discount brokerage house, I test whether the securities these investors purchase outperform those they sell by enough to cover the costs of trading. I find the surprising result that, on average, the securities they purchase actually underperform those they sell. This is the case even when trading is not apparently motivated by liquidity demands, tax-loss selling, portfolio rebalancing, or a move to lower risk securities. I examine return patterns before and after transactions."

"Return patterns before purchases and sales can be explained by the difficulty of the search for securities to buy, investors' tendency to let their attention be directed by outside sources, the disposition effect, and investors' reluctance to sell short."[20]

In another study, Professor Odeon discovered the following:

"Modern financial economics assumes that we behave with extreme rationality, but we do not. Furthermore, our deviations from rationality are often systematic. Behavioral finance relaxes the traditional assumptions of financial economics by incorporating these observable, systematic, and very human departures from rationality into standard models of financial markets."

"This paper highlights two common mistakes

[20] ***Do Investors Trade Too Much?*** by Terrance Odean, Graduate School of Management, University of California at Davis, 2/24/00.

investors make; they tend to disproportionately hold onto their losing investments while selling their winners, and they trade excessively. We argue that these systematic biases have their origins in human psychology. The human desire to avoid regret causes investors to sell their winners while holding their losers; the tendency for human beings to be overconfident prompts them to trade excessively."[21]

While working with many investors over the years, I have discovered that most of them seem to make the same emotionally driven mistakes. In order to overcome these mistakes, I recommend that you use a system. Let me explain what I mean by a system. There are many, many systems that work. Let me show you one that is very, very simple. It's one among many systems that possess these traits:

- There are no decisions to make
- The system tells you what to buy and sell
- The system tells you when to buy and sell

It sounds simple, so why do people use financial advisors and money managers? Mostly because, if advisors/managers explained every system in detail to their investors, most people would not stay with a system. They would get nervous during down markets and react to items in the news. So, it's well worth it for most investors to use a financial professional who is emotionally unattached and can keep them on a consistent program.

So if you want to stay on a system, have someone do it for you. Smart physicians do not operate on themselves, and in the same vein, people should not manage their own money. Your emotional reactions will likely cause you to buy and sell

---

[21] *"The Courage of Misguided Convictions: The Trading Behavior of Individual Investors"* by Brad Barber and Terrence Odean, ***Financial Analyst Journal***, November/December 1999, pp. 41-55.

at the wrong time. Humans were not designed to be good investors and that's why there are so few. At least a professional, who is handling your finances and the finances of others, can act based on logic and not emotional reaction.

Let's look at a simple system. The following table contains a list of 30 companies in the Dow Jones Industrial Average. Most of them are well-known household names—DuPont, Kodak, Intel, General Motors, etc.

Table 4.1
30 Stocks in the Dow Jones Industrial Average

30 Stocks of the Dow Jones Industrial Average

Philip Morris	General Electric	Aluminum Co Amer
AT&T	Kodak	Johnson & Johnson
JP Morgan	Caterpillar	Citigroup
Microsoft	Merck	Boeing
ExxonMobil	Home Depot	IBM
General Motors	SBC Communications	Coca Cola
International Paper	American Express	WalMart
MMM	Proctor & Gamble	Hewlett Packard
DuPont	United Technologies	Disney
Intel	Honeywell	McDonalds

Barrons, January 1, 2001

Here's a system that only uses the 30 stocks listed above. Regardless of what you read in the newspaper, you can generally always feel pretty good about owning these types of companies. In this system, you buy stocks for 10 out of 30 of the companies with the highest dividend yield and hold them for a year. At the end of the year, you should look to see if you still have ten stocks with the highest yields. If not, you should change the original ten to include the ten highest yields. You should do that every year. With this system how do you make decisions? You make selections based on the numbers.

Notice that you don't do any research on General Motors, and you don't read the newspaper. You follow the formula and never deviate from it. If you invested $10,000 in the market with S&P 500 companies (the major indicator of the market) over 29 years, your investment would be worth $265,199. No complaints and not bad. However, if you invested using the system I just explained and only bought those ten high yielding stocks, you would have had about twice as much in the same time period. By investing a similar system and buying only five stocks, called the DDS5, you would have had about four times as much money.

Remember that past performance is not a guarantee of future results. You can see from Table 4.2 that using a very simple formula can help you do extremely well. However, the key is to stay on the system. Unfortunately, most people can't. That's why people need to have advisors do the investing for them.

Table 4.2
Dow Dividend Strategy Performance Summary

	Standard & Poors 500	Dow Jones Industrial Average	Dow Dividend Strategy Ten	Dow Dividend Strategy Five
Value of $10,000 invested Jan 1, 1973	**$265,199**	**$287,624**	**$791,116**	**$1,485,289**
Average Annual Return 1973-2001	**12.0%**	**12.3%**	**16.3%**	**18.8%**
Standard Deviation (Risk)	**17.0**	**16.4**	**15.7**	**19.3**
Risk Adjusted Return	**0.70**	**0.75**	**1.03**	**.97**

Beating the Dow Newsletter, the Hirsch Organization and www.dogsofthedow.com. The Information presented has been obtained from sources believed to be reliable, but its accuracy is not guaranteed.

The use of compounded average annual total return and growth of $10,000 are presented for comparison purposes only. They are not intended to be either an expressed or implied guaranty of actual performance. Securities do not offer a fixed rate of return or risk. When sold, redeemed, or matured, they may be worth more or less than originally invested. With stock ownership comes more risk as market conditions change, companies are bought or sold, and even natural disasters occur that create volatility in the stock markets. Total returns do not take into consideration any sales charges, commissions, expenses, or taxes. The S&P500 and the Dow Jones Industrial Average are unmanaged indexes and cannot be invested in directly. None of the above information reflects an actual portfolio but rather different strategies for investing in stocks purchasing shares on January 1 and rebalanced one year later.

As with any investment methodology, the Dow Dividend Strategy cannot protect against loss or guarantee a profit. Please consult your investment representative before investing. The Dow 10 Strategy is documented in 'Beating The Dow" by Michael O'Higgins. The strategy standard deviation over this period is 15.7 vs. 17.0 and 16.4 for the S&P 500 and the Dow Jones Industrial Average, respectively. The table above represents a $10,000 hypothetical investment made in 1973 and employing the strategy continuously for 29 years. The table assumes that all dividends during the year are reinvested at the end of the year and does not reflect the impact of commissions (which may vary significantly from firm to firm), taxes (which vary from investor to investor) or expenses. The table is a fair comparison among strategies depicted as any of the above portfolios would be burdened by a comparable management fee and minimal trading costs. This fact applies to tables 4.3 and 4.4. However, the next table provides specific information on the effect of those costs on the Dow 10 Strategy. Past performance is not a guarantee of future results. In any given year, the strategy may show negative or positive performance and it may not be suitable for all investors. Note that these are hypothetical returns from following a system, not an actual portfolio. Also note that capital gains taxes are due when shares are sold at a profit and the stock dividends are taxed as ordinary income. Risk is measured above as return divided by standard deviation

Why can't people stay on such a system? I'll tell

After assessing a 1% annual management fee at the end of each year and 0.25% for trading commissions, the returns of the Dow 10 Strategy would have been as follows:

	Before management fee and commissions	After Management fee and commissions
Compounded return 1 years	-4.9%	-6.2%
Compounded return 3 years	1.6%	.03%
Compounded return 5 years	7.1%	5.9%
Compounded return 10 years	13.4%	12.1%
Compounded return 15 years	14.2%	12.9%
Compounded return 29 years	16.3%	15.0%
Ending value 12/31/2002	$791,116	$576,621

you very simply with a couple of good examples. In 1992, every time you turned on the radio you heard about cigarette smokers suing the tobacco companies. Now, you have good judgment, but would you have bought stocks in a tobacco company? No. However, the formula above said to buy Phillip Morris. Well, the formula told you to do it, so you did it and didn't listen to the radio. Over the next four years, Phillip Morris tripled in value. Of course, this will not always happen in your favor. But I want to illustrate the point that the news is not a good source of investment advice. In July 2000, Philip Morris had a $70+ billion judgment levied against them by a Florida court. By the end of the year, the stock rose 61% while the market was flat.

Now that may make no sense to you, because you think the market should work differently than it does. Here's another example. In 1990, we were in the middle of a recession. Every time you opened the newspaper you saw stories on General Motors temporarily closing another plant. They closed a dozen plants that year, laying off thousands of people. Now of course if you hear that news and the formula tells you to buy General Motors, you say, "I can't buy General Motors. Every time I open the newspaper it's bad

Table 4.3 Dow Dividend Strategy Annual Performance

Year	Standard And Poor's 500	Dow Jones Industrial Average	Dow Dividend Strategy Ten	Dow Dividend Strategy Five
1973	-15	-13	4	20
1974	-26	-23	-1	-5
1975	37	45	56	65
1976	24	23	35	41
1977	-7	-13	-2	6
1978	7	3	0	1
1979	18	11	13	10
1980	32	21	27	41
1981	-5	-3	8	4
1982	21	26	26	42
1983	23	26	39	36
1984	6	1	6	11
1985	32	33	29	38
1986	18	27	35	30
1987	5	6	6	11
1988	17	16	24	22
1989	31	32	26	10
1990	-3	-1	-8	-15
1991	30	24	34	62
1992	7	7	-8	23
1993	10	17	27	34
1994	1	5	4	8
1995	37	36	36	30
1996	25	29	28	26
1997	33	15	22	21
1998	28	18	10	12
1999	21	27	4	-4
2000	-9	-4	6	-12
2001	-11	-5	-5	-3

news." However, three years later, General Motors started running three shifts a day and couldn't meet the orders from the dealers. What I want to indicate is that most people cannot stay on a system because their emotions get the best of them. They read or hear something and end up taking themselves away from the system.

There's another reason why I like this system for conservative investors. Conservative investors are more oriented to protecting their principal than making it grow. There are certain stocks that tend to go down less when the market goes down—at least in past history. In 1973 and 1974, do you remember waiting in line for gasoline? The stock market went down over 41% in those two years. If you had owned the ten high-yielding stocks, then you would have made about a 3% profit.

It happened again in 1977. The market was down 7% that year. If you would have owned the ten stocks, you'd be down 2%. In 1981 we had a little bit of a dip in the market and it was down by 5%. If you would have owned the ten stocks, you would have been up by 8%. There has been one exception—in 1990. The market was down 3%, and the ten stocks were down 8%. So, six out of seven years over the last 29 years, when the market's been down, these stocks have either gone up or been down 50% less.

Table 4.4
Comparison of S&P 500 Stocks and Dow Dividend Strategy Ten Stocks During Down Markets

Year	S&P 500	Dow Dividend Strategy Ten
1973	-15	+4
1974	-26	-1
1977	-7	-2
1981	-5	+8
1990	-3	-8
2000	-9	+6
2001	-11	-5
Total	-76	+2

I cannot guarantee any system will make an investor profits, but I do know from experience with my own funds and millions of dollars of client accounts that patience and a system has improved the chances significantly. There are many good systems like this one with a structure for what to buy and when to buy and sell.

5

ANNUITIES

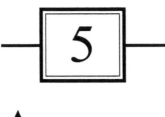

It's my observation that as investors age, they look for ways to save taxes on their investment income because they do not have earned income to shelter from taxes. Investments that provide some tax relief are annuities.

However, there are some mistakes that people often make when dealing with annuities. First, if you're going to pay estate taxes, never die with annuities or IRAs (If you're single and your estate is worth more than $1 million or you're married and your estate is worth more than $2 million, estate taxes will be due. (This estate exemption amount rises through 2009 under current law). In general, you want to avoid holding IRAs and annuities at death because those investments are the only two that are double taxed. Your heirs will pay the income tax and they'll also pay the potential estate tax. The total tax bite could climb over 70% on these assets.

Lots of seniors have purchased annuities for their simplicity and income tax deferral. Yet some annuity owners lose half of their annuity value and most aren't even aware of this!

Let's take a look at how this happens with a hypothetical example.

Mary, age 55, purchased a fixed annuity for $50,000. She held it for 10 years and the interest accumulated nicely. The account doubled to $100,000 (a compound rate of 7.17% which could have been locked in 10 years ago per data from *Annuity Shopper Magazine.*) So far, Mary was very happy with this alternative. She never gave much thought to what happens to the annuity at her death. She figured she would eventually withdraw the money and use it.

The truth is, less than 10% of the annuity owners I meet make any withdrawals from their annuity. If the owner passes away, the policies can get hit with some very large taxes. In Mary's case, here's the picture at the time of death when the taxes are due.

Annuity Value	$100,000
Income Tax	-17,500
Estate Tax	-33,000[22]
Beneficiaries get	$ 49,500

In the blink of an eye, Mary's beneficiary loses $50,500—over half of the annuity value! Is there a remedy? YES! If you do not plan to use the annuity for yourself, you can make a smart move with the following tactic:

Annuitize the annuity (deferred taxes or sales charges could apply or 10% tax penalty if under age 59½—please call for a review of your contract.) When you annuitize the annuity, you select a payout option that may include a lifetime income from the annuity company. You trade the $100,000 balance for a guaranteed income for life (or any period you choose.) (The shorter the period, the higher will be the monthly income paid to you.) If you want to know how much monthly income you can receive, please phone with your balance and age and I will send you a printout of your monthly income.

Mary had her insurance company make monthly payments to her of $700. She did not need the money, so she used the after tax amount to purchase a life insurance policy on her life, payable to her beneficiaries. Based on Mary's current age of 65 (and assuming she is a preferred non-smoker female), this $700 ($585 after taxes)[22] per month purchased her a $364,140 universal life policy.

Now, instead of Mary's heirs getting only $49,500 at her death (the amount that they would have received after the taxes on the annuity, as I showed you on the previous page), the heirs receive $364,140 of life insurance death benefit, free of estate and income tax![23] That's 7 times as much money for the beneficiaries, over $300,000 more!

Let's say you start the payments from the annuity as I described. For each payment you receive from the annuity, you are paying for the life insurance. Even if you died after the first premium on the life insurance, your beneficiaries would still receive the entire $364,140 death benefit on the life insurance policy.

---

[22]This analysis may not be accurate for every annuity owner as some people do not pay estate taxes. We assume a federal and state **combined** income tax bracket of 35% which may be higher or lower than your actual tax bracket. Estate taxes are assumed at 40%. A single taxpayer with taxable income over $65,500 will have a federal income tax bracket of 30% and a 5% state tax bracket in high tax states such as California. Note that estate taxes are paid by people with estates of $1 million+.

[23]We can explain the additional estate planning required to keep the proceeds of your life insurance policy out of your estate so that it passes **free of estate taxes**. Additionally, you need to qualify medically and financially for the life insurance coverage. This suggestion may not be beneficial in all cases. It depends on your income and estate tax bracket.

[24] Deferred annuity price trends from www.annuityshopper.com; 9.4% rate in November 1988 had declined to 4.7% in 2002.

Figure 5.1
Fixed Annuity Interest Rate Trends

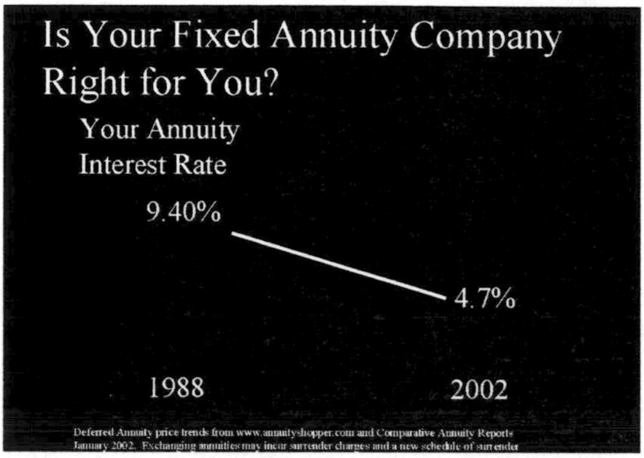

Is Your Fixed Annuity Company
Right for You?
Your Annuity
Interest Rate
9.40%
4.7%
1988
2002
Deferred Annuity price trends from www.annuityshopper.com and Comparative Annuity Reports
January 2002. Exchanging annuities may incur surrender charges and a new schedule of surrender

The second mistake that people often make with annuities is going to sleep on them. Many people purchased fixed annuities a while ago. The rate was good, say 9-10%. Now that same annuity pays you 4.7%.[24] You don't need to stay with the same company! You can switch to a company that will pay you more and get a locked-in rate, rather than one that changes. Section 1035 of the Internal Revenue Code says that you may switch from one annuity to another without payment of taxes. You may have surrender charges if you switch, but you may not (each individual annuity is different and must be checked). But it's an important issue to look at because why would you sit there year after year earning less than you could?

With variable annuities, which have values that rise and fall with the investment markets (based on the investment accounts you selected) there is a different issue to attend to. Of course, make sure your investment selections are performing to your satisfaction or else switch them in the same annuity or switch to a different annuity company.

Variable annuities also have a death benefit. Let's say you invest $100,000 and the investment account you select declines, causing your account to now be worth $80,000. If you die, your heirs get the $100,000. That's the death benefit. Therefore, you want to get the death benefit reset as often as you can in a rising market. In some variable annuities, it resets automatically—every five years for example. In other situations, you need to take action by reinvesting with the same annuity company or even switching to another company to get your death benefit reset.

By the way, this death benefit is not free. Investors often look at variable annuities as simply buying mutual funds on a tax-deferred basis. However, that is not so. You are getting an insurance contract and you are also paying for it. In fact, you have the investment account expenses (explained in the previous section on investment fees) that I will estimate at 1.5%. Then, you have expenses of the insurance wrapped around the investment accounts. This is typically another 1.25%. So you are paying 1.25% annually to get the tax deferral. (Note that loans, withdrawals and expenses reduce the amount of death benefit.)

Some studies indicate that you are better off in mutual funds and paying the taxes each year. Other studies show that the 1.25% cost is worth the tax deferral. The reason studies are inconclusive is because the better alternative (variable annuities vs. mutual funds) is affected by the following things:

- How great the fund turnover and how much tax is generated.
- The nature of the tax (long-term vs. short-term gains).
- How long you plan to hold the investment.
- Your tax rate today and your tax rate when you withdraw funds.

Many times, investing seems black and white. Once you learn more, you realize that more variables are involved and you can still come up with the best alternative, but it takes some analysis to do so. Back to the issue of switching annuities. This ability to switch may come in useful. The following cases are some examples that I have encountered over the years.

1. Mr. Jones, a retiree, had done well with his variable annuity. He wanted more safety and switched to a fixed annuity (which guaranteed his principal).

2. Mrs. Smith had a fixed annuity, which she had no intention of using. She wanted it to grow as much as possible. She switched to a variable annuity and selected stock sub-accounts.

3. Mr. Smith had a fixed annuity. He wanted to turn it into income. I checked with his current company that offered him $100 per month for life. Another company offered $120 per month for life, so I switched him to the company that paid him more.

4. Mr. Brown had a variable annuity. The fluctuations made him nervous, but he liked the growth. He switched to an index annuity, which guaranteed his principal but also gave him some stock market growth (more about index annuities in a moment).

There can be many reasons to switch, and you may be better off. Of course, a thorough analysis should be done before making any switches.

In the last five years, the insurance industry has come out with *index annuities*. With this option, you get interest each year based on the change in the S&P 500 (i.e. based on how the market does). However, if the market goes down, you don't lose any money. So, you get the upside, but not the downside. You will generally earn less with an index annuity as compared with a variable annuity in a rising market. However, you can incur losses in a falling market with a variable annuity, but not so with the index annuity.

If you have variable annuities and are concerned with preserving their values (assuming they are old enough and you don't have any surrender charges), you can switch from a variable annuity to an index annuity and not worry about losing any principal—note that the principal guarantee is from the issuing insurance company and is therefore subject to the claims-paying ability of the insurer.

Let's illustrate an example of an index annuity. It could have the following features:

- 100% of your original principal is guaranteed by the issuing insurance company.
- You get a 4% minimum guaranteed rate of return regardless of stock market performance.
- You earn 70% of the performance of the S&P 500 index over the next seven years.

So, you do not earn as much as being 100% exposed to the stock market as you could in a variable annuity. But, if you are concerned about capital preservation, the index annuity guarantees your principal, while a variable annuity does not.

Please note that this is a generic simplified comparison. Many variable and index annuities have other features too detailed to explain here. In the example on the previous page, if the S&P 500 did not advance or decline during the entire term of the annuity, the annuity holder would receive the minimum guaranteed rate of return--3% annually, less any expenses. (Also note that withdrawals made prior to the vesting period may cause any and all gains to not be realized.)

6

Income Investing

It's common that people desiring income will invest in bond funds. That's a fine alternative, but bond funds are a lot different than individual bonds and you should know the difference. If you want income, the primary instrument for getting income is a bond. You've got two choices—you can buy individual bonds or you can buy a bond fund. Let's take a hypothetical example—a ten-year bond that pays 8%. What's your interest rate the first year? 8% of course. What's the interest rate the fifth year? 8%. And the tenth year? The same.

Table 6.1
Comparison of Bonds Versus Bond Funds

Bonds	Bond Funds
Principal Returned at Maturity	No Maturity – No certain return of Principle
Interest Rate Fixed	Interest can Fluctuate

Note the other differences between individual bonds and bond funds:

Funds provide diversification.
Funds provide professional management.
Funds provide liquidity.

So the rate is fixed regardless of changes in the economy, the stock market or other variables. If you buy a bond fund and it starts out paying 8%, what's your rate the first year? Hopefully 8%. How about the second year? The rate can go up or down. Therefore if you want a fixed rate of income, a bond fund cannot be counted on to supply that. Bond funds do have some advantages, however, as indicated on the table above.

What about the principal? A bond can be sold at any time. However, since the price fluctuates, you may get back more or less than you paid. You know that you receive face value if you hold the bond to maturity. So the recommendation about buying bonds for conservative investors is to buy them and hold onto them until maturity. That way, you receive a fixed interest rate that you know in advance and you get face value at maturity.

On a fund, you do not have a fixed rate and since a fund has no maturity, there is no face value to recover. You will receive the market value of the shares, resulting in a gain or loss when you sell. I am not recommending that bonds are better than bond funds. I am simply recommending that you understand the difference so that you do not end up dissatisfied with what you receive.

Other Options

Before you renew your CD at the local bank, consider the fact that some banks out of your area may pay more interest. These banks are FDIC insured, the same as the bank in your neighborhood. But many banks do not have branches in each town and this can save them a lot of money. As a result, they can pay you more. Check with any knowledgeable financial advisor and you can likely find options for CDs that pay more than you may be accustomed to. (Although we have never encountered a CD that was not FDIC insured, always verify that the bank you select is FDIC insured.)

You may be able to do even better with another conservative investment—Collateralized Mortgage Obligations. With this investment option, you make a loan (just like all bonds you're making a loan along with a group of other investors and you're all lending your money at the same time) to an institution and the institution then lends the money out to homeowners to buy homes.

A federal agency such as Fannie Mae, Freddie Mac or Ginnie Mae guarantees your security. You don't need to worry about whether the homeowner pays his/her mortgage or not. You will get your payment each month whether the homeowner pays or not because the federal agency or federally chartered corporation guarantees your principal and your interest.

In fact, these securities have an "implied" AAA rating. Although they do not have formal ratings from the rating agencies, many investment professionals consider these securities to have a quality similar to those with an AAA rating, because of the federal agency guarantee as to payment of principal and interest. These securities have one significant difference as compared to treasury securities—the term of these securities is not fixed.

Let me give you an example. The average homeowner in the United States moves every seven years. So, you would expect that if you lent money to people to buy homes, you would get paid back in seven years, on average. However, when you lend your money in this fashion, it gets spread out and lent to many, many homeowners. Your money gets diversified. Some of those people are going to move in two years, some will move in five, but some are going to be in their homes ten, fifteen and twenty years from now. Therefore, when you make this type of investment, you will be quoted an estimated life of your investment, which may be five years, seven years, eight years or more. That's nated time for when you can expect the money to be d. Keep in mind that it is only an estimate and can change significantly. Therefore, you could incur costs of reinvesting and could be at the mercy of market swings.

There are many factors that I won't go into here, but just know that if you buy a Fannie Mae security or a Collateralized Mortgage Obligation that's guaranteed by Fannie Mae, and it has a five-year estimated life, you could see principal back in two years if some people, who borrowed the mortgage money, move very quickly. Other people will live in their homes for years and your money will continue to come in over the entire period. So you need to be prepared for that. Remember, that at all times your principal is guaranteed and you are receiving the fixed rate of interest that was promised to you at the beginning of the investment on any principal you still have working. As long as you're investing part of your core capital in these types of securities, you could have a potentially attractive return. Not a bad place to permanently park some money.

Let's close up this section by taking a look at bond mutual funds. An investor can purchase individual bonds as I have discussed or he/she can purchase a portfolio of bonds in mutual funds. This is merely a personal choice. Some investors like owning individual bonds because they want to know exactly what they own, when it comes due, what the rating is, etc.

When you purchase a bond fund, you are really purchasing the bond manager. Since the portfolio changes constantly, you will not know which bonds are in the fund. In fact, the maturity range of the bonds can change quite a bit. If the fund manager thinks that interest rates are falling, he may position the fund into longer-term bonds (20 years or more). Under the opposite expectation, the manager might shorten the maturities to under ten years. Therefore, if you want more control and more precision in the bonds you own, individual bonds would suit you better than a fund.

How do you find the bond fund that's right for you? You first need to decide, "Do you want government bonds, tax-free bonds, corporate bonds (mostly for IRA or pension), or convertible bonds?" Once you decide on the category, a financial advisor can use one of the many research services, such as Morningstar or Wiesenberger, to help you select the funds with favorable profiles. Once you select funds, remember to read the prospectus carefully before investing or sending money.

Preferred Shares – Another Income Source

Corporations raise money by issuing preferred shares, which are very similar to bonds. The big difference is that preferred shares have no maturity date. Once you invest in preferred shares, you own them until:

1. You sell them.
2. They are called by the corporation.

Why do investors purchase preferred shares instead of bonds? Generally, preferred shares pay a higher rate—generally 1% more income than bonds of the same company. The higher rate is due to higher risk in severe cases. If the company ever had financial problems, the bondholders would get paid first, before the preferred shareholders. Since the preferreds are second in line to be paid if the company liquidates, the preferred shareholders take more risk and are paid better. As a practical matter, if you buy high-quality preferred shares (these are ranked by S&P just as bonds are ranked), such companies are not likely to go into liquidation.

Generally, preferreds are issued at $25 per share. You can invest in these shares when they are first issued or anytime by purchasing on the stock exchange. Make sure that you check the call feature. I have seen many investors buy preferred shares that pay a high current dividend. However, what they did not realize was that they bought the shares at $30 and the call feature allowed the company to call the shares the following year at $25. These investors experienced a whopping $5 per share loss because they did not check the call feature.

Preferreds pay dividends every quarter. For investors who want to have their income keep pace with current market conditions, there are adjustable rate preferreds. These shares do not have a fixed dividend, but rather have a dividend that is usually based upon treasury bill/bond rates. As the interest rates move up or down in the economy, so will the investor's income. There is usually a minimum and maximum rate that is guaranteed. So if you find a minimum rate that is attractive, you can invest and sit tight when interest rates rise and potentially collect more income.

Table 6.2
Examples of Preferred Shares

S&P Rating	Description	Symbol	Div Rate	Next Payment	Price	Current Yield	Yield to Call	Call Date	Call Price	
AA	Sun amer Cap II 8.35%	SAIprw	0.5218	9/30/01	25.49	8.19%	0.41%	11/12/01	25	8/13/01
A+	ABN AMRO Cap Fund II 7.125%	ABNprB	0.4453	9/30/01	24.94	7.14%	7.22%	3/31/04	25	8/13/01
A+	Farmers Group 8.25%	FIGprB	0.5156	10/2/01	25.34	8.14%	8.12%	12/31/25	25	8/13/01
A+	Texaco 6.875 MIPS	TXCprA	0.4296	11/1/00	24.88	6.91%	13.32%	any	25	8/13/01
A	Chase Preferred 8.10%	CMBpr	0.5062	9/30/01	25.38	7.98%	-7.78%	9/17/01	25	8/13/01
A-	Allstate Fin 7.95% QUIPs	ALLprA	0.4968	9/30/01	25.26	7.87%	4.20%	11/24/01	25	8/13/01
A-	Duke Capital Fin II 7.375% QUIPs	DUKprU	0.4609	9/30/01	25.4	7.26%	6.56%	9/30/03	25	8/13/01
A-	Travelers P&C 8.08%	TAPprA	0.505	9/30/01	25.25	8.00%	**	any	25	8/13/01
BBB+	Capital Re LLC 7.65% MIPs	KREprL	0.4781	11/1/01	21.75	8.79%	**	any	25	8/13/01
BBB+	Mediaone Fin 'B' 8.25% TOPR	UMGprY	0.5156	9/30/01	25.25	8.17%	3.40%	10/28/01	25	8/13/01
BBB+	Public Storage 8.875%	PSAprG	0.5546	9/7/01	24.89	8.91%	**	any	25	8/13/01
BBB	American Annuity 9.25%	AAGprT	0.5781	10/16/01	24.99	9.25%	9.41%	11/6/01	25	8/13/01
BBB	Sierra Pacific Power 8.60%	SRPprT	0.5375	10/2/01	25	8.60%	**	any	25	8/13/01
BBB	Lincoln National 8.35%	LNCprY	0.5218	10/2/01	25.2	8.28%	**	8/20/01	25	8/13/01
BBB	AT&T Capital Corp 8.25%	NCD	0.5156	9/30/01	25.5	8.09%	7.28%	11/15/03	25	8/13/01
BBB	Nexen 9.75%	NXYpr	0.6093	9/15/01	26.4	9.23%	7.00%	10/30/03	25	8/13/01
BBB	NVP Capital I 8.20%	NVPpr	0.5125	9/30/01	24.95	8.22%	8.52%	4/1/02	25	8/13/01
BBB	Equity Residential Trust 8.6% D	EQRprD	0.5375	9/30/01	26.95	7.98%	6.98%	7/14/07	25	8/13/01
BBB-	Placer Dome 8.625%	PDGprA	0.539	9/28/01	24.35	8.85%	16.51%	12/17/01	25	8/13/01
BBB-	Gables Residential Trust 8.3%	GBPprA	0.5187	8/29/01	25	8.30%	8.30%	7/24/02	25	8/13/01
BBB-	BRE Properties 8.5%	BREprA	0.5312	9/30/01	25.46	8.35%	7.67%	1/28/04	25	8/13/01
BBB-	Newscorp 8.625%	NOPprA	0.539	9/30/01	25	8.62%	**	any	25	8/13/01
BBB-	Taubman Centers series 8.3% A	TCOprA	0.5187	9/30/01	19.93	10.41%	27.59%	10/3/02	25	6/21/01

These are not recommendations.

7

IRAs

The Big IRA Mistake

Many investors pay a great deal of attention to how they invest their IRAs, but ignore the "end game." The end game is when the IRS splits the IRA with you through taxation.

First, do not designate your living trust as your beneficiary. This will cause your IRA to be immediately taxable in full upon death. Always name a person (or an irrevocable trust) as beneficiary. By naming a person or irrevocable trust as beneficiary, your beneficiaries gain the possibility of deferring the IRA distributions and the taxes for many years.

Second, realize that the smart thing to do for income taxes could be the dumb thing to do for estate taxes. Most people have it in their minds to defer income taxes as long as possible. Therefore, if you do not need to use all of your IRA, then you want to pass it along and have it benefit your heirs for as long as possible. That makes perfect sense as far as income taxes go. But what about estate taxes?

At this writing, an estate is taxed once it exceeds $1 million in value. (This exemption amount rises to $3.5 million in 2009. Please note that even though *current* law increases the exemption over time, there's nothing to stop the next Congress from bringing the exemption down again. It's politics, you know).

In your effort to pass on the largest IRA balance to your heirs, you could give up 50% of it to estate taxes under current rates. You'll be even worse off if your IRA is most of your estate. The estate tax could be due with no other cash to pay the tax. The heirs will be forced to liquidate part of the IRA and pay income taxes for the purpose of paying estate taxes! What to do? Read on for a solution.

Ready to Retire? Don't Miss This Huge Tax Savings!

Many retirees have employer stock in their 401(k) and profit sharing plans. In these cases, there is an opportunity for converting ordinary income (which could be taxed at rates up to 38.6%) into capital gains income (taxed at only 20%).

Here's how. Rather than rolling over the employer stock into an IRA, take actual distribution of the shares. You will pay tax (at ordinary income rates) on the basis of that stock (the basis is the value of the shares when they were originally put into the plan). When you eventually sell the shares, you will be taxed on the unrealized appreciation as a capital gain. If you rolled-over the shares into an IRA, you would pay ordinary income tax on the entire value of the shares as they are withdrawn from the IRA.

Let's look at an example. Joe has a 401(k) plan at ABC Manufacturing. He invests his contributions into company stock during his tenure—a total investment of $100,000. When Joe is ready to retire, the shares are worth $600,000. Let's first assume that Joe rolls over the shares into an IRA. He then reaches age 70½ and must begin taking distributions from his IRA and paying taxes on those withdrawals at ordinary income rates (up to 38.6%). He will pay these full rates on all of his shares. Assuming no further appreciation above the $600,000, Joe would pay taxes of $231,600 on the shares (at the 38.6% rate).

But let's assume that Joe read this chapter and does not roll over the shares. He takes them as a distribution and pays taxes of $38,600 immediately on the basis (38.6% of $100,000). Later, he decides to sell the stock (at his discretion because he is not subject to the 70½ rule as the shares are not in an IRA) and he pays capital gains tax of $100,000 (20% of $500,000). His total tax bill is $138,600 rather than the $231,600 he would have paid had he rolled his shares into an IRA. That's a cool savings just shy of $100,000—enough to pay for plenty of great vacations for Joe and his wife.

Are you retiring in the next three years? Don't miss out on many planning opportunities that may not be explained by the mutual fund companies or your CPA.

Don't Put That in an IRA!

Here's a simple idea that can save you significant taxes. Place certain assets in your IRA and leave other assets out of your IRA. (Note that this discussion pertains to traditional IRAs and not Roth IRAs.) You should place assets that have the highest tax bite in an IRA. For most taxpayers, these income assets include CDs, bonds, bond funds and many mutual funds. These assets, which generate ordinary income and short-term capital gains, have their income taxed at the highest rates (e.g. federal rates up to 38.6%). By placing these in an IRA, you defer these high taxes as long as possible.

Keep stocks out of your IRA. Long-term capital gains are taxed at a maximum of 20% for stocks outside of your IRA. But if you place stocks inside of your IRA, when you eventually remove the money, it will get taxed at regular rates, since IRA withdrawals are always taxed as ordinary income.

Are you paying more taxes than necessary? Do you have the right assets in your IRA? Check your investments against the way they are taxed to make sure you have the right investments in the right spots.

Age 70? Taking Minimum IRA Distributions?

I meet many people who have reached age 70½ and are taking only the minimum required distributions from their IRAs. By taking only the minimum requirement, their income taxes are minimized. But this tactic can create another problem. If only the minimum amounts are being taken, the IRA balance continues to grow and it could be subject later to double taxation—income and estate taxes.

For example, an IRA owner age 70 has a 16-year life expectancy.[25] Assume he has a $100,000 IRA and takes only the minimum distributions each year and the IRA earns a hypothetical 10% annually. By life expectancy, that IRA balance will be $215,233. If our IRA owner's total estate exceeds $1 million (this exemption amount rises through 2009), then the remaining IRA balance could be subject to income tax and estate tax, which could exceed 70% under current law.[26]

By taking only minimum distributions and saving taxes today, our investor could create a huge estate problem for tomorrow. Can this be avoided? Yes. Instead of taking only the minimum distribution, our IRA owner can take an additional $7000 annually (and pays the additional tax of $2450 based on a 35% tax bracket out of this $7000) and invest the remaining after-tax amount of $4550 in a hypothetical life policy owned outside of his estate.

---

[25] ***IRS Publication 590***, 2000.

[26] Assuming a combined state and federal income tax of 35% and estate tax of 50%.

Now, at his life expectancy, rather than leaving his heirs an IRA balance of $100,000+ that would be subject to combined taxes exceeding 70%, his heirs receive a death benefit of $170,000, which is free of estate and income taxes. The family just increased its net worth by $106,102.[27]

If your current plans will result in leaving an IRA to your family, you can leave them a lot better off if this technique fits your situation.

How Your IRA Could Face an 80% Tax

Large IRAs face the double whammy of income and estate tax. Without proper planning, the combined tax could exceed 80%. ***The Individual Retirement Account Answer Book*** by Panel Publishers illustrates an example of a $2 million IRA exposed to all kinds of taxes.

NY State Death Taxes (16%)	$ 320,000
Net Federal Estate Tax (39%)	$ 780,000
Net Income Tax (43% Combined Rate)	$ 533,099
Total Taxes	$1,633,099
Beneficiaries Receive (18.3% of Original IRA)	$ 366,901

What can you do?

1. Take distributions from your IRA and spend it.
2. Take distributions from your IRA and make gifts ($10,000 per year per donee or $20,000 per donee if you are married).

[27] The difference is between the tax-free death benefit of $170,000 and the $215,233 subject to a 70% tax of $150,663. Note that this analysis is not accurate for everyone since not all taxpayers are subject to estate tax. Note that there may be fees and expenses associated wiht purchase of life insurance.

3. Take distributions from your IRA and contribute as premiums for life insurance and have the tax-free death benefit offset the above taxes.
4. Use your IRA (rather than other assets) for charitable bequests or to establish a testamentary charitable remainder trust.
5. Distribute your IRA and contribute the balance to a charitable family limited partnership to offset the tax.
6. Use the Pension Asset Transfer Strategy to rescue your IRA (see *www.pension-asset-transfer.com* for more details).

The ***Kiplinger Retirement Report*** of August 1999, offers the following advice: Plan for estate taxes. If you have a large IRA and few other liquid assets, consider using required distributions to pay for second-to-die life insurance premiums. This insurance pays on the death of the second spouse and is usually owned by an irrevocable life insurance trust or the IRA's beneficiary so that insurance proceeds stay out of your estate. (A single person can also use a life insurance trust to pay estate taxes). "Whatever you take out of the IRA for premiums, you've removed from your taxable estate and replaced with an estate tax-free asset," points out Edward Slott, a CPA in Rockville Centre, New York.

If this could apply to you, do not wait. The IRS is very happy to take taxes from people who procrastinate. Any one or combination of the above options is better than leaving your IRA as tax fodder. (See Appendix C for an interesting article entitled, *"A Change in the Rules"*).

8

ESTATE PLANNING

The Ways Many People Mess Up Their Living Trusts

Many people do the right thing by having a living trust prepared. After all, why would anyone subject their heirs to a lengthy, costly and needless probate process? But these same trustees fail to investigate how to make the most of the trust and feel that the "job is done" once they have their trust completed. In fact, many people make enormous errors, which can be extremely costly.

Error #1: Leaving assets outright to heirs. The trusts that I see leave assets outright to heirs, which means that the heirs are free to squander the assets and the heir's creditors are free to attach these assets. In other words, many people have instructions in their trusts that when they die, the assets are distributed to the heirs outright. Wouldn't it make more sense to leave assets to heirs in trust so that they will be protected from outside forces and so that you can also control the squandering of the assets? Additionally, by leaving assets in a trust, they can be kept out of the heirs' estates, so as to avoid estate taxes again. It's an often observed phenomena that the next generation dissipates the wealth created by the parents. In my observation, the parents are sometimes contributors by leaving the assets to heirs outright.

I suggest a simple process whereby your living trust has assets placed in a *bypass trust* at your death. That bypass trust continues indefinitely, for the entire lives of your children (and can even continue for additional generations). The income from the trust can be distributed to your heirs and you can leave precise instructions for when and how the principal can be distributed (e.g. to buy a house or to start a business or at age 60, etc.). While assets remain in this bypass trust, they enjoy protection from creditors and also family disputes. Your son or daughter may have a great marriage today, but if divorce occurs and the assets you have left get commingled, your daughter-in-law or son-in-law may have a claim to these assets. If the assets are in trust, no claim can be exercised.

Error #2: Failure to manage the bypass trust correctly. When one spouse dies, a bypass trust is created and funded with assets of the deceased spouse. Many people give no thought to which assets to place in the bypass trust and how they should be managed. Selecting the right assets is very important for tax reasons and wealth creation. Assets in the bypass trust should have two objectives—grow as much as possible and generate no taxes. In fact, I see these assets managed incorrectly most of the time in the following way:

The surviving spouse invests the bypass assets to generate income for their own benefit. At the same time, their own assets are growing in value (e.g. stocks and house) and become subject to estate taxes. This makes no sense. In fact, the surviving spouse should spend down their own assets to ensure that those assets will be below the estate taxable level, while allowing the assets in the bypass trust to grow as much as possible. In other words, many people do just the opposite with the assets in order to minimize tax and maximize wealth creation.

In fact, one of the best uses of a bypass trust is to use it as an *irrevocable life insurance trust.* Such an arrangement can pay off several times to the heirs through completely tax-free life insurance benefits. In this case, some or all of the assets in the bypass trust are used to purchase a life insurance policy for the heirs' benefit. When the second parent dies, the life insurance pays off, providing a potentially large payment to the heirs. This payment is free of estate and income taxes. Depending on the parent's age and health when the insurance policy is obtained, the proceeds to heirs could realistically be 200% to 600% of the premium invested.

Error #3: Selecting the wrong successor trustee. I see many parents select one or all of their children as successor trustee(s). This can be a formula for disaster and create hard feelings among siblings, misunderstandings and even costly mistakes if the children are not business savvy. I always encourage selecting an independent trustee who is knowledgeable in estate matters and can settle an estate efficiently. An attorney, accountant or financial advisor is a good choice.

Table 8.1
Scheduled Estate Tax Exemption Per Person

Year	Amount
2002	$1,000,000
2003	$1,000,000
2004	$1,500,000
2005	$1,500,000
2006	$2,000,000
2007	$2,000,000
2008	$2,000,000
2009	$3,500,000

Reminder: Congress can change the above figures at any time.

The $500,000 Mistake

I get calls every week from investors wanting to know the best place to invest money. It's a reasonable question, but I often find that the investor is focused on the wrong part of their financial situation. Does it really matter if an investor can get a 12% return rather than 6%, if they ignore their estate planning situation and pay the government an unnecessary $500,000? (A married couple with no estate planning and an estate of $2 million will pay estate tax, under current rates, of $502,050. It is not uncommon to find retirees who have appreciated investments and real estate with estates over $2 million.) Wouldn't it make more sense for an investor to focus on the best way to save that $500,000 rather than focusing on how to invest $50,000 to earn another $3000 per year? The answer is obvious, but it's not how many people behave.

Why do investors behave in this way? Most investors incorrectly believe that estate planning is about giving money away and losing control over their assets. This mistaken perception is promoted by attorneys and advisors who provide shallow advice about simplistic strategies of gifting money away or giving it to charity.

For example, a common recommendation is to place money in an irrevocable trust in order to remove it from your estate. That common suggestion means you lose control. If these advisors really kept current with their fields, they would also know that money can be made exempt from estate taxes while still giving you access to the funds. You do not need to lose control. In other words, assets can indeed be placed in an irrevocable trust, which removes them from your estate and from estate taxes. That same trust can also contain provisions for providing distributions to your spouse (if your spouse needs them) or loans back to you if you need the assets.

If you listen to many advisors, it sounds like estate planning is about relinquishing control of your assets. When in fact, estate planning is about maintaining control of your assets. Just look what happens if you do not utilize estate planning—the government takes control over your money and here's how they spend your estate taxes:[28]

- Defense (17%)
- Interest on National Debt (11%)
- Physical and Community Development (9%)
- Social Programs (49%)
- Law Enforcement (2%)
- Surplus to Pay Down Debt (12%)

If you don't like how the government spends your money, estate planning will redirect how your money is spent, based on your desires. Therefore, estate planning is about taking maximum control of your money—assets that can be directed based on your desires, not the government's desires.

Other reasons why investors fail to do estate planning include just plain ignorance and mistakes in their knowledge. Some investors still think that if they have a living trust, they'll pay no estate taxes. This is a widely held misconception. Other investors hate talking about estate planning because they'll have to confront mortality. As mentioned before, some investors think that estate planning means giving money away. In fact, good estate planning starts with making sure you have ample resources for yourself. Good estate planning makes sure that you pay less income taxes today, have increased income and can possibly liquidate assets without capital gains tax. Estate planning is for you, as well as the next generation.

[28] ***2001 IRS Instructions Form 1040.***

Some people think that their estate planning problem will go away because the government is raising the level on the estate tax exemption (the exemption is equal to $1 million per person in 2002, rising to $3.5 million in 2009). Don't forget however that the Government giveth and taketh and the next Congress could easily lower the exemption. Since dead people don't vote, the estate tax is the easiest tax to levy.

Estate planning boils down to one simple issue—do you want to have control of your money? How do you start? I start by having clients complete a questionnaire that helps them focus on their goals and desires. The questionnaire is followed up by an interview to help translate the answers into specific desires. Only then do I go to work to determine ways to achieve what my client wants. This practice avoids the common mistake that many people make—they jump right into the tools (trusts, gifting, insurance), only to learn later that the tools don't work as desired.

So if you really want to make a big difference in your financial picture, it may make more sense to focus on estate planning, rather than spending time trying to get a higher percentage on your investments (a percentage that the government may get most of anyway).

A Solution to the Estate Tax Dilemma

It's unbelievable that families still pay estate tax. Estate taxes are voluntary and can be avoided. Yet, every year, the IRS collects billions in estate taxes from families whose parents did nothing to eliminate the tax ($29.7 billion in 2000).[29]

One reason some parents do not act is because they are advised to shrink their estate through gifting. This gifting

[29] ***IRS Estate Tax Returns*** filed in Fiscal 2000.

obviously removes assets from their estate (making them poorer) and thereby lowers the value of the estate and the estate taxes.

Parents often resist gifting for fear of giving up the assets, losing the liquidity and maybe someday needing those assets. Well there's a way for parents to have their cake and eat it, too. It's called the WRAP Trust™ (WRAP stands for Wealth, Retirement and Asset Protection).

The WRAP Trust™ is an irrevocable trust with the following benefits:

1. Assets (life insurance, cash and investments) can be removed from the estate and placed in the trust.
2. The parents can borrow from the trust and the loan needs never to be repaid during the parent's life-time (the parents are in effect, borrowing from themselves).
3. The assets in the trust are protected from creditors.

The parents retain their liquidity because they can borrow from the trust at any time, yet the assets are removed from the estate and from the reaches of the IRS. This is a far more flexible arrangement than the typical "life insurance trust" recommended by many advisors.

If you will have an estate exposed to taxes (current value $2 million for a married couple), then setting up a WRAP Trust™ can be the solution.[30]

---

[30] (The WRAP Trust™ is a trademark of James Blase, JD, LLM St. Louis, Missouri.)

What Is the Most Common Estate Planning Mistake?

The most common estate planning mistake involves spouses who hold property as joint tenants. Generally, that's a bad idea and here's why. If you and your spouse hold assets as community property, when one spouse dies, the other spouse can sell the property without taxes (all prior capital gains are erased). But if the property is held as joint tenants, the deceased party has the capital gains erased on his half but capital gains tax is due on the other half sold by the surviving spouse. Therefore, eliminate all capital gains tax by holding appreciating assets with your spouse as community property.

You can easily change the title on your assets. For your house, you can usually get the right form at your county recorder's office or a title company. For securities, simply notify your brokerage firm that you desire a change and they will open a new account with the right title.

What about joint tenancy with your kids? Bad idea. If your son is in a car accident and gets sued, the plaintiff can come after the assets you hold jointly with your son and force the sale of that asset.

Simple estate planning mistakes can have BIG costs. The following basic rules serve most people well: Avoid probate by using a living trust, not by titling assets in joint tenancy. If a living trust is not used, a husband and wife should hold appreciating assets as community property. If a living trust is not used, some States allow probate to be avoided by placing a beneficiary name on securities and real estate. Check with your title company and securities firm for more information.

You do not need a living trust to avoid probate in many cases. Many people want to avoid probate—the court process, which divides your estate based on your will or state law. Some people title their assets in joint tenancy, because joint tenancy avoids probate. But this action can create problems. Joint tenancy can create a gift, which needs to be reported on a gift tax return. More importantly, you expose the asset to the legal liabilities of the other party. Say your son, a general contractor is involved with a building and someone gets hurt. They sue him and attach his assets. The asset you own in joint tenancy with your son is placed at risk.

The solution is a living trust, which avoids probate and will not expose your assets to any other person's liability. However, the simplest way for small estates may be the Pay On Death (POD) and Transfer on Death (TOD) provisions available in many states. These provisions allow you to name a beneficiary on bank accounts, securities and real estate. That way, the asset passes directly to the named beneficiary.

However, you need to be careful. If your will says that your house is to be divided among your three children, but the TOD provisions in your deed says that only one child is named as beneficiary, your will has no effect and the named beneficiary gets the house. Additionally, you need to watch out for how your will deals with estate taxes. If the taxes are to be divided equally among the heirs, the three children will share the tax on the house that only one child inherited.

This Expert Says It's a Big Mistake

Among estate planners, Stephen Leimberg is considered a foremost expert. He is a JD, CLU and professor of taxation and estate planning at the American College in Bryn Mawr, PA. He is an attorney, a nationally known speaker and a best-selling author of more than 40 books on estate, financial and retirement planning. More than 40,000 attorneys and estate planners subscribe to his newsletter. I wanted to share the following quotation from his article on, *"The Ten Most Common Estate Planning Mistakes."*

> *"Mistake 10: Lack of a "Master Strategy" Game Plan. Do-it-yourself estate and financial planning is the closest thing to do-it-yourself brain surgery. Few people can do it successfully...A key principle in estate planning is that you can't eliminate the big mistakes in your estate plan until you've identified them."*

Many people think that they have done the right thing, but the mistakes I see are common. Here is one of the most common mistakes—appointing your child to act as your executor or trustee. In an article by Stephen Leimberg and Charles Plotnick, *"Selection of Executor, Trustee, and Attorney,"* they say that you should consider many aspects in selecting a trustee. Some of these features include:

- Availability
- Impartiality and lack of conflict of interest
- Financial security
- Investment sophistication, policy and track record
- Business sophistication
- Accounting and tax-planning expertise
- Record keeping and reporting ability
- Decision-making abilities
- Competence
- Integrity
- Flexibility to meet changing circumstances
- Experience as a trustee

I still hear many stories about parents who are supporting their children financially, yet have selected their children as trustees of their trust. Does a grown adult child who needs financial help meet the above standards?

If you have done nothing more than had an attorney draw up a living trust, then this is hardly estate planning. You or your heirs could still be exposed to estate taxes, unnecessary income taxes and improper distribution and liquidity problems in settling your estate. The best thing you can do is select a knowledgeable trustee to handle the trust when you are gone.

Get That Life Insurance Policy Out of Your Estate

Do you own a life insurance policy? Not a good idea. It's fine to have life insurance to protect your family or pay off estate taxes, but you never want to own it. Your life insurance policy should be owned outside of your estate.

Your life policy has a surrender value (the amount you get if you cash it in) and a death benefit (the amount the beneficiary gets when you die). Even though the surrender value is the real value to you, the IRS will levy estate tax on the entire death benefit if this policy remains in your name (in your estate).

Let's take a step back. A life insurance policy has three parties:

> **The Owner**—the person who controls the policy and has legal ownership.
> **The Insured**—the person whose life is insured.
> **The Beneficiary**—the party who gets the death benefit when the insured dies.

Many people automatically have the same party as the owner and the insured. This can be a costly mistake. In a typical situation, it would be best to have the parties set as follows:

> **The Owner**—the children or irrevocable life insurance trust.
> **The Insured**—you.
> **The Beneficiary**—the children or irrevocable life insurance trust.

By setting the parties as above, at your passing, the policy is not in your estate and will not be subject to estate taxes. How do you get a policy out of your estate? You could gift it to your children or to an irrevocable trust that you establish for the benefit of your children. If the cash value is less than the estate exemption amount ($675,000 currently rising to $3.5 million in 2009), there is no tax to make the gift.

You will however use up some of your estate tax exemption if the amount of the cash value exceeds your $11,000 annual exclusion ($22,000 if married). But don't die for three years! The IRS will pull the death benefit back into your estate if you die within three years after gifting a policy. Some people will make the gift and then buy a three-year term policy to pay the estate taxes on the policy should they die within the three-year window.

Your other alternative is to sell the policy to your kids. When you sell the policy, the three-year rule discussed above does not apply. However, the IRS has set up another trap. The policy is exposed to the "transfer for value" rule. Since the policy was paid for, when the eventual death benefits are paid to the children, they will be taxable (normally, death benefits are tax free).

You can escape from the transfer for value rule if you and your child are business partners. You can easily become partners by each buying a share in a publicly traded master limited partnership (traded on the stock exchange). Tricky? It can be. Consult a professional before removing a life insurance policy from your estate.

Book Summary

I would like to end this book with some words of advice about investing that will serve you well. The opportunity of a lifetime comes along about once per week. Ignore hot tips or "time urgent" investment opportunities. Do not act on the news. Watch television financial shows and listen to them on the radio, but do not act on what you hear. Rather, listen to each expert and notice how they say things opposite to what others say. So who's the real expert? Remember that commercial television and radio stations exist to sell ads, and you should never rely on them for investment decisions.

Do not watch the market. Invest and go to France for ten years. Based on history, an investment in the S&P 500 was profitable in 97% of the ten-year periods since 1926. Great investing requires great patience.

Do not do it yourself. Managing your own money is a formula for disaster, because you are emotionally driven. When someone else handles your investments, they have the opportunity to make decisions based on logic. The fact that you have an opinion (deny it if you will) at this moment regarding the stock market's direction is an indicator that your emotions, prejudices or something you heard on the news is influencing you and stripping away all logic.

Think in long horizons and organize your investments to last a lifetime. Follow a course that not only makes sense, but feels comfortable. It's difficult to profit when you are changing investments frequently. In order to hold on for the long term, you must be comfortable with your program. In other words, set up your program based on a comfortable risk level, not based on how you think you can make the most money.

I would be delighted to answer any of your questions that have not been addressed in this book. You can call me directly or write down your questions and fax or mail them to me. I might have additional brochures or booklets that could help you make important decisions about your finances.

Michael Pultro, RFC
PO Box 5210
11 Iroquois Avenue
New Britain, PA 18901

Phone: (215) 489-3876
Fax: (215) 489-3839
Email: pultro@snip.net
Website: www.michaelpultro.com

About Michael Pultro

Michael Pultro has been assisting senior investors since 1987. He is a well-known financial educator in the Bucks & Montgomery County area. His unique retirement and asset preservation seminars have been very popular among retirees and those about to retire who want to protect their assets and provide for a secure lifetime of income. In his practice he has counseled numerous people on avoiding the common mistakes often made by retirees. He has helped many people cut income taxes, avoid taxes on Social Security, increase spendable income and reduce or eliminate estate taxes.

Michael Pultro is a Certified Senior Advisor, which required him to take a 23 section course of study and pass a rigorous exam proving his comprehensive knowledge of personal retirement and lifestyle issues as they apply to seniors. Michael is also a Registered Financial Consultant that required a college degree and a minimum of 10 years of experience in the financial planning industry.

Michael lives with his wife Kim, who is a dance instructor and his 2 sons Tate & Tyler. Michael's hobby , when he is not helping retirees improve their financial lives, is playing tennis at the Doylestown Tennis Club and coaching soccer.

He retained an industry expert to write and compile the information in this book. His goal is to better educate the people he meets and hopefully make them better managers of their own finances, help them avoid common mistakes and provide them with options to hopefully secure their financial future.

APPENDIX A

Star funds often burn out quickly

Most that reach No. 1 ranking not even average in subsequent years

ERIC TYSON

YOUR MONEY MATTERS

EVERYBODY LOVES A winner, especially when it comes to investing their money.

With mutual funds continuing to boom and now managing in excess of $3.7 trillion dollars — and dozens of publishers telling us which funds are tops in various categories and time periods — there's no lack of top funds competing for our attention.

However, investing in recent top performers could be hazardous to your wealth.

Working with the mutual fund research firm Morningstar, I analyzed how an investor would have done over the past 15 years if he or she had bought yesterday's star funds -- that is the stock and bond funds which achieved the coveted No. 1 performance rankings each year.

The surprising result: Over the subsequent three-, five- and 10-year periods, a whopping 80 percent of these "star" funds performed worse than the average similar fund. Some No. 1 funds have ended up at or near the bottom of future performance charts.

When I first started following the financial markets back in the mid-1970s, the stock market suffered a stunning 45 percent drop

[*See TYSON, Page B-2*]

Republished with permission of The San Francisco Chronicle; permission conveyed through Copyright Clearance Center, Inc.

Appendix A

TYSON from B-1

Star funds often burn out quickly

in less than two years.

Following this bear market, the Dow Jones industrial average had a strong 38 percent recovery in 1975. The 44 Wall Street fund (which has since been renamed the Matterhorn Growth fund) surged ahead a whopping 184 percent in 1975 and was the top performing U.S. stock fund of that year. Money gushed into the fund after this stunning rise.

But investors who bought into 44 Wall Street based on its strong short-term performance ended up with disappointing results.

In the 1980s, one of the best decades ever for the U.S. stock market, the 44 Wall Street fund held the dubious distinction of being the single worst U.S. stock fund. And recent years haven't treated this fund much better.

Over the most recent 10-year period, the average annual rate of return for the fund has been just 7 percent, less than half the market's average of more than 15 percent.

Other examples of fallen "stars" can be found among the fund managers who first scored by loading up on high-flying technology stocks.

San Francisco money manager Garrett Van Wagoner was considered the small-company stock mutual fund manager with the hot hand.

Around the time Van Wagoner launched his own fund management firm in late 1996, several of the nation's largest financial magazines recommended investing in his new Emerging Growth fund.

In a piece last spring entitled Rookies of the Year, a major magazine featured this "promising new fund" managed by a "stellar" manager.

The Van Wagoner Emerging Growth fund opened its doors to new investors at year-end 1996 and the cash came flooding in — more than $1 billion in its first six months. Unfortunately for investors, Van Wagoner's fortunes quickly took a turn for the worse late last spring.

Van Wagoner made some big bets on market sectors such as technology stocks that did poorly over the past year despite the market's continued rise.

In fact, over the most recent 52-week period ending May 23, the Van Wagoner Emerging Growth fund performed worse than 1,801 out of 1,807 U.S. stock funds. The total return was down 30.4 percent, compared with a 27 percent total return in this period by the Standard & Poor's 500.

Money has since flowed out of the fund. According to Morningstar, investors yanked more than $150 million out of the Emerging Growth fund between last October and this April.

"Van Wagoner has taken as big a hit as anyone investing in growth company stocks with momentum. Basically, he was a one-man show early on but he added analysts recently to help with research. He certainly works hard and knows his companies," says Larry Chin, associate editor of the Orinda-based investment newsletter "No-Load Fund Analyst."

The relatively poor performance of many of yesterday's star funds shows the dangers of fund investors focusing heavily on past performance in purchasing funds.

Here's how to find the funds most likely to deliver solid returns in the years ahead and avoid buying into a skyrocketing fund on the verge of turning back toward Earth:

► Remember that very high returns are correlated with taking great risks.

Risk and return go hand in hand. Funds that deliver extreme returns — either positive or negative — are the ones that employ the riskiest investment strategies.

With stock funds, a typical way a fund manager can increase risk is by weighting the portfolio heavily in one or two industry sectors.

Another way is to buy into so-called momentum stocks that already have soared on the hopes that the trend will continue.

► Don't buy a top-performing fund unless you are prepared to see your fund possibly at or near the bottom of future mutual fund performance charts.

Be sure to examine how the fund manager has done in down or changing markets.

► Understand how those high returns were achieved.

When Van Wagoner was managing money at the Govett Smaller Companies fund in 1995, for example, his fund had a turnover ratio of 519 percent, meaning that he held his individual stocks on average about 10 weeks.

If that rate of trading makes you nervous, then that's a sign you should be investing in stock funds that are doing longer-term investing.

Van Wagoner also racked up the lion's share of his market-beating returns over at his prior fund when it had less than $100 million under management, which allowed his concentrated industry bets to really shine when they were correct.

The legendary Fidelity Magellan fund achieved its top returns during Peter Lynch's tenure in the late 1970s and early 1980s when the fund was much smaller and invested heavily in smaller-company stock that greatly outperformed larger stocks.

By 1993, Magellan's assets swelled above $30 billion and, after several manager changes, the fund has lagged the market averages ever since.

► Do an apples to apples comparison with comparable funds.

Top-performing funds' return numbers usually don't look as extraordinary when you compare those numbers against those of funds with similar investment strategies.

For example, in recent years, the domestic stock market has, on average, performed much better than foreign markets. Thus, any mutual fund that markets itself as a foreign fund but in fact has had a good chunk of money invested worldwide, including the United States, has had an unfair advantage when its performance is stacked up against true foreign funds.

► Read the fund's recent annual reports to see what types of investments a fund really holds. Also consider checking in with Morningstar, whose reference publications can be found at most public libraries.

Morningstar's single-page fund write-ups include a thoughtful analyst commentary as well as an analysis of the fund's holdings.

► Investigate the overall reputation and track record of the parent company.

When you're considering investing in say the American Century International Growth fund, in addition to checking that specific fund out, also examine what other international funds American Century runs and how they've done over the years.

► Pay more attention to fees than past performance. Over the years, the vast majority of mutual funds earn close to the market average returns.

However, funds differ greatly in the fees — sales commissions and ongoing operating expenses — that they charge investors. All things being equal, higher fees translate into lower returns.

In fact, the single best predictor of a fund's future returns is not its past returns but the fees that it charges. Remember that high fees indicate either a small fund which is more costly per dollar invested to manage or a fund company enriching itself at your expense.

Eric Tyson, author of the best-sellers "Personal Finance for Dummies, 2nd edition" and "Investing for Dummies" (IDG Books), will teach an 8-week money course at the San Francisco campus of UC-Berkeley Extension beginning June 11.

Appendix B

FRIDAY
MARCH 14, 1997

TIMES BUSINESS

SECTION C
INSIDE
➤ Work & Family 2
➤ Stocks 4
➤ Dividends 5

CVSW

Dow plunges 2.3%, rates rise sharply

By DAVID BARBOZA
New York Times

NEW YORK — Stocks plunged Thursday in the steepest selloff since July as interest rates rose sharply and caused more investors to question whether the market had become too expensive.

The Dow Jones industrial average plummeted 160.48 points, or 2.3 percent, to close at 6,878.89. While the drop was the fifth-largest point decline in Dow history, it did not even rank in the top 50 declines in percentage terms.

The drop in stock prices was widespread, with declining stocks beating advancers by almost 4-to-1 on the New York Stock Exchange.

"It was a very pervasive, sweeping decline," said Michael Metz, chief investment strategist at Oppenheimer & Co., and a longtime bear. "It's the worst I've seen in months, and I think it's the beginning of something more serious, because valuations are stretched to the limit."

Yet even as most stock indexes fell Thursday, the mutual fund industry was reporting that cash inflows into equity funds remained strong in February. The Investment Company Institute, a trade group, said equity funds netted $19.5 billion last month, well below the record January intake of $29 billion, but still

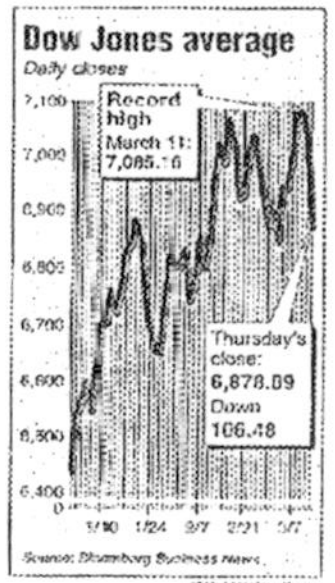

the seventh-largest figure in history.

Having broken the 7,000-point level last month in record time, with gains of more than 1,700 points, or about 32 percent, since last July, some believe that the Dow and the broader market — which is already in one of the longest bull runs in history — have been long overdue for a correction.

And while few analysts were willing to declare the beginning of a bear market Thursday, several said that the economy's continued strength was raising fears that inflationary pressures could lead to higher interest rates that would slow the economy and unhinge an ebullient stock market.

Indeed, Thursday's decline seemed to have been set off by rising interest rates in the bond market following a report that retail sales this year had risen much more strongly than expected. As a result, many more analysts said the Federal Reserve Board would almost certainly raise short-term interest rates at its policy meeting March 25.

On Thursday the yield on the benchmark 30-year bond rose to 6.96 percent from 6.88 percent on Wednesday, reaching its highest level in nearly six months. And as yields rise, analysts believe that money will flow out of stocks and into bonds, which become more attractive. In addition, earnings expectations could decline as interest rates rise and threaten to slow economic growth.

"If we hold at 7 percent, the market will find its footing," said Richard Cripps, chief market strategist at Legg Mason. "But if we go above 7 percent, then we'll have more downside."

While the benchmark yield had approached the 7 percent level earlier this year, analysts said that Thursday's large rise — about seven basis points — was quite dramatic.

"The key factor here is that the bond market and the stock market are intertwined," said Byron Wien, the U.S. investment strategist at Morgan Stanley. "The retail sales numbers sent the yield up eight basis points, and that's a lot in one day. And if the market's already overvalued, a move like that emboldens the indecisive and makes them more willing to sell."

And sell they did. Of the Dow's 30 component stocks 28 lost ground Thursday. Only AT&T, which ended unchanged at 35⅞, did not fall.

The Dow's big loser Thursday was Philip Morris, which plunged 10⅜, to 126, accounting for nearly one-fourth of the Dow's losses.

Analysts attributed the decline, in part, to a decision by the Mississippi Supreme Court, which ruled Thursday that the state could proceed with its lawsuit against tobacco companies.

If your dogging the Dow, just hold on

By MARA DER HOVANESIAN
Staff writer

First the Dow Jones industrial average is rescued, then it tumbles. If you're a so-called "Dog of the Dow," holding the highest yielding stocks of the 30-company index, you might be tempted to bail out. But stay dogged.

"The best thing to do is just to sit tight," said Chris Orndorff, senior vice president and portfolio manager for Los Angeles-based Payden & Rygel. "After you've held it for a year, re-balance the portfolio. The strategy is predicated on holding those stocks for a 12-month period."

The Dow Dividend Approach to investing seeks to beat the well-respected index by selecting the top 10 yielding stocks, then investing equal amounts in the five lowest priced and readjusting just once a year.

Orndorff says that investors who trade stocks more often than that will realize a lower annualized return over time. Also, high turnover means investors will lose the tax deferred benefit of long-term capital gains.

"The short-term capital gains for individual investors can be substantial particularly when it's compounded over time," he added. Payden & Rygel's four-month-old Growth & Income Fund, a mutual fund tied to the Dow and Standard & Poor's 500, has grown from $2 million when it started to $45 million today. The simulated one-year return, says Orndorff, is about 24.8 percent.

The moral is that Dow Dividend investors should wait (usually until January) to switch their Texaco stock, which will be dropped Monday from the blue chip index to make room for Caterpillar stock. The other new Dow additions — Hewlett-Packard, Johnson & Johnson, Wal-Mart and Travelers Group —

Please see DOW, Page 8C

APPENDIX B

THE TIMES

BUSINESS

TUESDAY, MAY 6, 1997 Stocks • Finance • Investing *SECTION* C

BAROMETER

+143.29 STOCKS 7,214.49 Dow industrials at close

+$2.70 GOLD $343.00 Per troy ounce

-0.01% BOND YIELD 6.87% 30-year Treasury

Bay Area

Central Garden buys nursery supply firm

Lafayette-based Central Garden & Pet Co. on Monday announced the acquisition of Ezell Nursery Supply Inc., a Los Angeles County-based distributor of garden, barbe-

Dow soars 143 to record high

Investor optimism credited with broad advance of stocks

By CHARLES STEIN

The stock market soared to record highs Monday, carried along by optimism about the economy, interest rates and a shrinking federal budget deficit.

The Dow Jones industrial average rose 143.29 or about 2 percent to close for the day at 7,214.49. The previous record high was 7,085.11. The Standard & Poors 500 Index also hit a new record high.

The Nasdaq Composite Index had the best day of all, continuing an explosive rally that lifted the technology-heavy index almost 8 percent last week alone. Monday the Nasdaq was up 33.91, or 2.60 percent, to close at 1,339.24.

"There is no question the bulls are running on Wall Street," said Robert Freedman, chief investment officer at John Hancock Funds.

The market got a lift late Monday afternoon when a jury in Florida ruled R.J. Reynolds Tobacco Co. was not liable for the death of a smoker. Fears about the closely watched case had depressed tobacco stocks.

After a month of nervousness, investors appear to believe that life is good again.

A series of economic reports last week suggested the United States was enjoying the best of all worlds: solid growth without very much inflation. The economy expanded at a 5.6 percent clip in the first quarter, the strongest growth in nine years. The jobless rate in April dipped to 4.9 percent, matching a 23-year low.

Typically that kind of strength would indicate a growing threat of inflation and potentially higher interest rates. But two key inflation measures last week showed wages and prices rising at a very modest rate. And there were signs — in softer car sales, weaker manufacturing orders and a dip in consumer confidence — that the economy may return to a more sustainable 2 percent to 3 percent growth rate in the second quarter.

Still more good news last week came out of Washington. President Clinton and Republican leaders Fri-

See DOW, Page C4

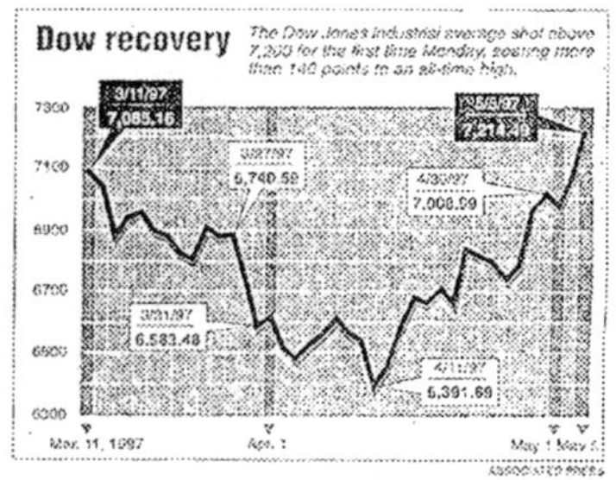

Republished with permission of The Boston Globe; permission conveyed through Copyright Clearance Center, Inc. .

Appendix C

A Change In The Rules

Surprise! Retired clients may save money by tapping qualified plans first.

By Tracey Longo

Money is money, right?

Not quite, planners and investors are learning, when it comes to spending hard-earned assets in retirement.

The rules of thumb for deciding which investments to tap first are changing, especially if clients find themselves in an upper tax bracket. For years, retirees have been told to spend their nontaxable assets first — the stocks, bonds and mutual funds they hold outside of their individual retirement accounts, qualified plans and variable annuities. Spending nonqualified money first, the thinking went, let retirees accumulate more in qualified plans as a result of tax deferral.

Sounds smart, but the problem for those in the 40% tax bracket is that they wind up paying out a huge chunk of earnings in income taxes when they take distributions from qualified plans. The tab for capital gains on nonqualified equities is only half that, a relatively mild 20%.

That has some experts recommending that retirees who expect to live 20 or 30 years in retirement not only preserve their nonqualified assets, but also start withdrawing those assets they have in qualified plans and IRAs and converting them to taxable equities.

"It's a sucker's bet for people in the 40% income-tax bracket to continue to defer in retirement," says Rick Adkins, principal of the Arkansas Financial Group, a financial advisory firm in Little Rock, Ark.

Let's say a client has $2 million sitting in a qualified plan when he or she retires. Assuming it will grow by 10% a year, the retiree will have about $30 million in 30 years. The new advice: It's better to pay 40% tax on the $2 million by taking the distributions early in retirement. That allows retirees to convert the assets to taxable equities, reducing the tax bill to a 20% hit for a pool of money that is likely to grow into a much bigger portfolio over the years, Adkins says.

Letting $2 million ride in a qualified plan can cost heirs even more. When you expire, they'll not only be required to pay income tax at the 40% tax rate, but they'll also get hit with the 55% estate tax on anything over $1 million (the estate-tax exemption that's being phased in over the next six years).

"It's a sucker's bet for people in the 40% income-tax bracket to continue to defer in retirement." Rick Adkins, Arkansas Financial Group

"We're definitely seeing an increase in clients who have a substantial portion of their assets in qualified plans and relatively little in taxable accounts," says Marilyn Bergen, president of Capital Management Consulting in Portland, Ore. "The higher the tax bracket, the more likely it is that a retiree will benefit from moving some portion of their account to taxable equities early."

The upshot is a 20% tax rate. From there, a retiree with charitable intent can create a charitable remainder trust, which provides income for life and even a tax write-off that can be used to offset other taxes. At death, the trust is transferred to the designated charity.

For those with wealthy children, a generation-skipping trust is an option that allows one's adult children to avoid estate taxes by earmarking the funds for grandkids. In generation-skipping trusts, up to $1 million can be excluded from estate taxes.

The point, says Adkins, is there is no one silver bullet that works for everyone. "Most people have to use a combination of means to achieve tax efficiency in retirement, so the earlier you get started, the better."

Reprint with permission from Financial Advisor Magazine .